Timesaver
For Real!
English in Everyday Situations

Teacher's reference key

A small clock on each page tells you approximately how long each activity should take.

Contents

Worksheets

Shopping

Entertainment

Contents

Communication

Travel

At School

Indexes

○ 0 = track numbers for audio component

Teacher's notes

Music Store: Store guide
Intermediate

1 & 2
- Elicit from students what music CDs they have bought recently. Get them to talk about how and why they made those choices.
- Individually or in pairs, students suggest what other products, apart from audio tapes and CDs, might be bought from a large music store, then compare their ideas with the store guide on the worksheet.
- Discuss what might be found in some of the categories, e.g. Hip Hop, Easy Listening, World, Children's, and invite questions on any items they don't understand.
- Give students between 5 and 10 minutes to do exercise 2.
- Students compare answers in pairs before class feedback.

Answers
1 chart compilations
2 gift voucher
3 exchange, refund
4 clothing
5 poster
6 budget

Cultural References
In Britain, the market for recorded music and home entertainment is dominated by a few retail giants such as Virgin and HMV. However, there are still many small independent 'record shops' which specialise in music audio, and in larger towns you can usually find good second-hand shops offering bargains or rarities for the collector.

Music Store: Music vocabulary
Intermediate

1
- Briefly explain about quizzes (see Cultural References below).
- Students can work in groups, looking at Jeff's answers and correcting them if necessary. The exercise calls for cultural as well as linguistic knowledge, so the emphasis should be on the communicative aspects of the task (discussion & sharing ideas).
- Extension: ask students to create their own music quiz. Each person writes one question which is put into a box. Teams are formed and the teacher takes out the questions one by one, and writes them on the board, making any necessary corrections to the language.

2
- Students can work in pairs, using clues in the sentences to identify the missing words.

Answers
1 1 folk
  2 soundtrack

3 reggae
4 heavy metal
5 world music
2 2 board game (picture f)
  3 lyrics (picture c)
  4 blank (picture b)
  5 headphones (picture a)
  6 playstation (picture d)

Cultural References
The quiz is a well-established institution in England: many pubs, small cinemas and other clubs have a weekly quiz night where teams of local people compete to answer general knowledge questions on subjects such as pop music, sport and cinema.

Music Store: Videos
Intermediate

1 & 2
- This exercise provides practice in punctuation and also presents some typical features of colloquial speech: short responses ('yes, she is'); fillers ('well, actually'); exclamations ('no way!') and vague language ('all that stuff about …').
- Ask students to practise the conversation with a partner with special attention to sentence stress, e.g. 'That's *very* good.' and 'No, she's not *that* young!' and intonation patterns e.g. the rising tone for suggestions 'What about …?"

Answers
A: No, she's not that young!
D: Well, what about *True Lies* with Arnold Schwarzenegger?
A: No way! She hates action movies.
D: Then perhaps she'd like this Harry Potter video?
A: No, I don't think so. She's not into all that stuff about witches and wizards and magic spells.
D: Your sister sounds difficult to please!
A: Yes, she is!
D: Does she like romantic films?
A: Yes, she does, actually.
D: Well, how about this one: *Shakespeare in Love*. It's about how the young poet got inspired to write *Romeo and Juliet*.
A: It sounds good. She has to study Shakespeare at school so this will be just right for her.

Teacher's notes

Supermarket: Supermarket layout
Intermediate

1

■ Optional introduction: before handing out the worksheet, read Bob's shopping list aloud, slowly. In pairs or groups, students try to recall and write down as many items as possible.

■ Give out the worksheet. Go through Bob's list with students. (See Language Notes below). Explain, or elicit explanations for the following vocabulary items: *curry* (a spicy dish originally from India); *punnet* (a container for fruit such as strawberries or nectarines); *free range* (farm animals that are allowed to feed and move around outside).

■ Students look at the plan of the supermarket and re-write Bob's list in a more logical order, so he doesn't have to go backwards and forwards to the same places.

2

■ Writing. Point out the variety of forms used to ask for directions, 'Excuse me, where can I find ...?'; 'Could you tell me where the ... is?'; 'Do you know where the ... is?'

3 & 4

■ Reading in pairs and controlled speaking practice. Students should aim to use the target language from memory, referring only to the supermarket plan.

5

■ Role play. Discuss what kinds of special offers and promotions supermarkets use to attract customers and increase sales, for example: two for the price of one, 20% extra of the product is free, free gift with the product purchased, theming (linking products with events or personalities in the news).

■ Divide students into groups of between 3 and 6. Each group has to brainstorm ideas for original offers/promotions and then choose one idea and develop it in more detail. They then choose one person in their group to present their idea to the class.

■ Teacher and whole class can vote or give feedback on the most original (and most practicable!) ideas.

Answers

1 A logical order would be: nectarines, plum tomatoes, carrots, Top of the Pops magazine, microwave meal, eggs, large wholemeal loaf, olive oil, cooked ham from the deli, milk, carton of fresh orange juice, salmon steaks, minced beef, honey-coated cornflakes, baked beans, crisps, sparkling mineral water, tutti frutti ice cream, Pepsi, coffee
2 3 In aisle 9, opposite tea and coffee.
  4 Excuse me. Could you tell me where the fresh meat is?

5 It's in aisle 12, opposite rice and pasta.
6 Excuse me. Where can I find fruit juice?
7 It's with the jam on the left in aisle 2, opposite yoghurt and eggs.
8 Excuse me. Do you know where the vinegar is, please?
9 Yes, they're near the entrance, opposite fresh fruit.
10 Excuse me. Where can I find Customer Services?

Language Notes

■ *semi-skimmed*: describes milk from which half the fat content has been removed
■ *honey-coated*: in the UK some varieties of breakfast cereals are sweetened with honey or sugar, making them very attractive to children in particular.
■ *decaffeinated*: describes coffee from which the ingredient caffeine has been removed, making it a milder drink.
■ *sparkling*: describes table water which is carbonated or slightly 'fizzy'. Contrast with *still* or *natural* water, which is without bubbles.

Supermarket: Vocabulary
Intermediate

1

■ Pre-listening: elicit from students a few examples of items that can be bought from a supermarket. To limit the range of possibilities, give categories, e.g. fruit; dairy; household; delicatessen.
■ Play the recording. Students write the missing words on the packaging of the items illustrated.

2

■ Students read through the true/false questions.
■ Play the recording again. Students compare answers in pairs before class feedback.
■ Recall exercise: from memory, students try to list all the new words and expressions which Nathalie learnt at the British supermarket.

Answers

1 a ginger
  b squash
  c cheese
  d spread
  e kitchenware
  f fruits of the forest
  g cutlery
  h fudge
  i dressing
2 3 True
  4 False. He loves it.
  5 False. She didn't buy any. (She wasn't sure what it was like).
  6 True
  7 True
  8 False. He thinks it'd be horrible if you didn't add water.
  9 False. Cutlery means knives, forks and spoons.

Teacher's notes

10 False. A cheese grater is an example of kitchenware.

11 True

12 True

Tapescript

D: Hello, Nathalie. How did you get on at the supermarket?

N: Fine. I think I got everything.

D: Did you find it very different from supermarkets in France?

N: Not really, though of course I didn't understand all the signs and labels. But usually you can see what a word means by looking at the product. For example I didn't know the word 'spread' but when I saw the box of Sunflower Spread, I understood it means a kind of soft margarine you can put on bread.

D: That's right, though actually we don't say box for the container, we say tub.

N: A tub of sunflower spread?

D: That's right. It sounds like the supermarket is a good place to learn new vocabulary!

N: Yes, really. I actually think it is. I also learnt the word 'dressing' today.

D: You mean 'surgical dressing'?

N: No, no. 'Dressing' as in 'salad dressing'. I didn't know it's the word you use for oil and vinegar mixed together to put on salad.

D: Right. What else did you learn?

N: Well, I discovered something called 'fudge'.

D: Mm, lovely. Did you buy any?

N: No, I wasn't sure what it's like. Is it nice?

D: I love it. It's a kind of soft sweet made with cream and butter, oh and sugar of course.

N: Very fattening, I expect.

D: Yeah, but it's really nice ... you can get it with nuts in or cherries or just plain. They say the best fudge comes from Devon.

N: Devon?

D: Yeah. In the south-west of England.

N: That reminds me – I also found out that you have loads of different English cheeses. I was really surprised – you never see them in France.

D: No, I guess not!

N: Cheddar seems to be the most popular, though – they had so many varieties: mature cheddar, medium cheddar, mild cheddar, West Country cheddar, Irish cheddar, even Canadian cheddar!

D: Yeah, but there's also Double Gloucester and Red Leicester and my own favourite Stilton. That's a blue cheese, but not too strong. You ought to try it.

N: Mm, maybe I will. Listen, I made a note of a couple of things I wanted to ask you.

D: Go ahead.

N: In the section for yoghurts, they had one flavoured yoghurt called 'Fruits of the Forest'. What does that mean?

D: Fruits of the forest? Oh I think it's supposed to mean wild berries, you know, like blackberry, raspberry, and blackcurrant. Blueberry too, I think.

N: Right. That's what I thought. And what about this. 'Squash' – S.Q.U.A.S.H. In the soft drinks section they had a bottle of something called Blackberry and Apple Squash.

D: It's pronounced squash.

N: Sorry, squash.

D: Well, it just means it's like a syrup, very thick, and you have to dilute it before you drink it.

N: You mean add water to it?

D: Yes. Otherwise it'd be horribly sweet!

N: Oh. And here's something else I learnt – knives and forks are called 'cutlery'.

D: Yeah. Didn't you know that? Knives, forks and spoons.

N: They had packs of 'disposable cutlery' – which just means plastic knives and forks.

D: The kind of thing you take on a picnic and throw away afterwards.

N: What a waste!

D: Yeah. Did you learn anything else at the supermarket?

N: Well, yes. I learnt the word 'kitchenware', which means all the tools you use in the kitchen such as a can opener or a cheese grater or a washing up brush.

D: Yeah, like the way we say hardware and software when we talk about computers.

N: Mm, I hadn't thought of that. Oh, something else I found is a beer with no alcohol in it.

D: Uh-huh?

N: Yeah, it's called ginger beer.

D: Oh, yeah. Well, that's not really beer, I mean it's more of a soft drink, it's quite sweet.

N: Well, I bought a few bottles. I'm going to try it. Would you like some?

D: OK. Why not? Here are some glasses. What do you think?

N: Phew ... it's hot, isn't it ... I mean sort of spicy.

D: Yes, of course. That's the ginger!

N: Oh ... I've just realized what it is. I mean I've just remembered the word in French. Of course! Mm. I quite like it, actually.

D: Better than boring lemonade anyway! Cheers!

N: Cheers!

Cultural References & Language Notes

■ a surgical dressing is a plaster or bandage that is put on a cut or other wound.

■ Cheddar, Double Gloucester, Red Leicester and Blue Stilton are among the most popular English cheeses. They are all named after the towns in England where they were first produced, though nowadays they are made in many different parts of Britain.

Teacher's notes

Packaging: Labels and instructions
Intermediate/Upper Intermediate

1

■ Introduction. If possible, show students some examples of real English language packaging. Instructions for electronic products are frequently printed in many different languages. It can be interesting to compare L1 version with English. Discuss the function of packaging: as means of attracting the eye of the consumer, and as a source of important practical information (size, weight, ingredients, price, etc.).

■ Give students 15-20 minutes to do matching exercise, using dictionaries if necessary.

■ Check answers.

2

■ Give students 5 minutes to do this second matching exercise.

■ Check answers.

■ Recall exercise: read the directions again in random order. Students write down the name of the product, e.g. 'Press to redial one of the last 5 numbers called' – telephone.

Answers

1 a 2; b 14; c 6; d 4; e 11; f 10; g 13; h 3; i 15; j 16; k 1; l 9; m 5; n 12; o 8; p 7
2 1 j; 2 k; 3 d; 4 e or g; 5 i; 6 b; 7 n; 8 c or h

Post Office: Sending things abroad
Intermediate

1

■ Begin by asking the students to talk about post offices in your own country – how you use them to send things to other countries – how much different things cost and if it costs more to send them to different parts of the world.

■ Ask students to imagine they are in England for a few weeks and that they need to send some things to friends and family. Elicit from them the kind of things they might want to send home or to friends in other countries – postcards, greeting cards, letters, pictures, photos, birthday presents, etc.

■ Elicit or ask students to use dictionaries to find the meaning of: weigh(t), abroad, posters, plus three more words from the lists of things in the first text.

■ Give students the text to look through quickly and ask any questions on items they don't understand.

■ Allow students 15-20 minutes to do the wordsearch and answer the questions. They could work in pairs on this.

■ Students can compare answers in pairs before class feedback.

2

■ Bring in a map of the world and elicit from students the names in English of the continents

and some of the major countries they know. You could ask who has visited the most countries and also find out who knows the names of capital cities, etc.

■ Ask students to read the text about zones and then, quickly to scan the list of airmail prices to make sure they understand it. Practise saying a few of the prices.

■ Allow students 10-15 minutes to do exercise 2.

■ Check answers.

Answers

1 2 weight; 3 calendar; 4 diary; 5 greetings card; 6 poster; 7 abroad; 8 postage; 9 goods
2 2 small packet, Europe, £1.83;
  3 small packet, Rest of the World Zone 2, £2.01;
  4 printed papers, Rest of the World Zone 1, £1.37 + £1.71 = £3.08;
  5 letters, Rest of the World Zone 1, 5 x £0.42 = £2.10;
  6 printed papers, Europe, £0.94;
  7 small packet, Rest of the World Zone 1, £2.07;
  8 printed papers, Rest of the World Zone 1, £1.89;
  9 printed papers, Rest of the World Zone 1, 2 x £2.07 = £4.14
  10 printed papers, Rest of the World Zone 2, 2 x £1.21 = £2.42, 2 x £1.21 = £2.42, 2 x £1.41 = £2.82 Total = £7.66

Post Office: A conversation
Intermediate

1

■ Introduce this by setting the scene and eliciting from the students what they might say in the post office when asking for stamps and sending different things home.

■ Play the recording once without the worksheet to check general comprehension – who, where, what she wants. etc.

■ Give students the worksheets and tell them to listen very carefully for the things that are different in the script. You will need to play the recording in sections, probably more than once. Allow time for students to confer in pairs and to write the corrections.

■ Check answers.

2

■ Play the recording again and stop after each phrase and sentence, asking the students to repeat. Pay particular attention to the pronunciation of prices and to aspects of connected speech.

■ Ask the students to try to reproduce the pronunciation, stress and intonation of the recording, reading the dialogue in pairs.

■ Ask students to switch roles. Then ask one person to cover their worksheet and see if they can say their half of the dialogue without reading. Switch roles, etc.

Teacher's notes

3

■ You will need the 'At the Post Office: Sending things abroad' worksheet for this exercise. When you are satisfied that the students are very familiar with the dialogue, go on to the roleplay and ask them to create their own dialogue.

■ Move students from pairwork, to small groupwork and finally to role-playing their dialogues in front of the class.

Answers and Tapescript

Cashier number <u>three</u>, please.
<u>Cashier</u> number <u>seven</u>, please.
Cashier: Good <u>morning</u>.
Laura: Hello. <u>I'd like</u> to send these postcards to Italy, please.
Cashier: How <u>many</u> have you got?
Laura: Let me see, <u>four</u>, <u>five</u>, and this one, <u>six</u>, please.
Cashier: <u>Six</u> at <u>thirty</u>-seven each, that's <u>two</u> pound <u>twenty-two</u>.
Laura: OK, and I've got this packet of <u>photos</u>.
Cashier: Is <u>that</u> for Italy too?
Laura: Yes, that's right.
Cashier: Can you put it on the <u>scales</u>, please?
Laura: <u>Here</u>?
Cashier: No, over <u>there</u>. That's one thirty-eight.
Laura: One thirty-eight. And these <u>English</u> newspapers too.... on the <u>scales</u>?
Cashier: Please...they weigh <u>400</u> grams so that's another two pounds and thirty three pence. So, altogether that comes to <u>five</u> pound <u>sixty-three</u> please. Thanks, <u>ten</u> pounds..... <u>four</u> thirty-seven change. Just <u>pass</u> the packet and papers through to me. Right.
Laura: Thanks, bye.
Cashier: Thank you.

Cultural References and Language Notes

■ *Queuing:* It is very important in Britain to join the queue if there are other people waiting in front of you. You must queue in shops, public places and when you are waiting for buses, taxis and trains. Most post offices and banks, etc. have a central queuing place, often marked 'Please queue here', and an automatic system with a lighted display and voice telling you when a position is free.

■ Shop assistants often use '*that comes to*' to say how much you have to pay when you have bought more than one thing. We can also use it to ask the total cost of a bill – *How much does that come to?*

1

■ Ask students to describe an item of clothing they bought recently, or their current favourite item. Where necessary, introduce language to describe clothes, e.g. *patterned, plain, baggy, tight-fitting, short-sleeved, sporty, smart*. Students can try to draw their item and label it. Discuss what styles are fashionable now, in tops, trousers, shoes, etc. You could bring in some photos cut out of fashion magazines; ask students to try to describe the garments shown in the pictures.

■ Look at the illustrations of clothes and shoes on the worksheet. Ask students to try to describe some of them.

■ Play the recording. Students listen and choose the correct picture.

■ Check answers and discuss, referring to illustrations.

2

■ Give students 2-3 minutes to read exercise 2. Play recording again.

■ Check answers.

3

■ Give students 5 minutes to do exercise 3.

■ Check answers.

4

■ Give students 5 minutes in pairs to find explanations for the 'odd one out' exercise.

■ Discuss possible answers with the whole class.

Answers

1 1 c; 2 a; 3 c; 4 a; 5 b; 6 b; 7 c; 8 a

2 2 breasted; 3 suit; 4 pattern; 5 tight; 6 flared, loose; 7 heels; 8 look fat; 9 plain; 10 matching; 11 hooded; 12 logo

3 2 suit; 3 go with; 4 try on; 5 size; 6 dressed; 7 wearing; 8 accessories; 9 rinse; 10 clothes, smartly; 11 sportswear

4 2 *shiny*: it describes texture. All the others are materials.
3 *tights* are worn underneath: the others are worn on top.
4 *a skirt* is a garment: the others are accessories.
5 *frilly* describes design: the others describe pattern.
6 *reduced* describes a cheaper price: the others describes size.

Tapescript

1 *A: What about this jacket here?*
  B: I don't like the fur collar.
  A: Then how about this double-breasted one? It'll go with your new trousers.
  B: No, I'd prefer a single-breasted jacket.
2 *B: How do you like this top?*
  A: I don't like halterneck tops, they don't suit me. I prefer this one with the round neck.
  B: Yeah, that's nice. I like the bead pattern on

Teacher's notes

the front.

3 A: *Look at these jeans.*
   B: *No, they're too narrow. I'm after some baggy ones.*
   A: *Flared, you mean?*
   B: *No, not flared, just baggy. You know, loose fitting and with pockets at the side, low down.*
4 A: *I need some shoes.*
   B: *What about these?*
   A: *No, the heels are too high.*
   B: *Do you want flat shoes, then?*
   A: *No, not flat, something in between – bit of heel but not too high.*
5 B: *This jumper's nice – why don't you try it on?*
   A: *No, it's chunky knit. It'll make me look fat.*
   B: *What about this – it's lambswool. Fine knit.*
   A: *Mm. That's better, but it's a roll neck. I want a V-neck jumper.*
6 B: *What about this track suit?*
   A: *No, I don't like the stars on the front.*
   B: *Well, what about this one with the stripe down the side?*
   A: *No, I've decided I want something completely plain. Like this one.*
7 B: *What can I get for Mum?*
   A: *What about a pair of gloves? Or a hat?*
   B: *A hat's OK, but it doesn't seem enough. I know – I'll get her a matching hat and gloves..*
   A: *Yeah – good idea.*
8 A: *How would you like this blouson jacket, it's nice soft material.*
   B: *No, it's old-fashioned. I'd rather have a hooded top.*
   A: *A hooded top? Well, there's one here.*
   B: *It's white! I want a dark colour. This one with the eagle logo is cool. Yeah, I think I'll take this.*

Language Notes
Language used to describe clothes, particularly fashion wear, changes rapidly, like the fashions themselves. However, some high-frequency words, like *top* for any miscellaneous t-shirt-like garment, have lasted a long time. Other words come back in as the fashions themselves are revived, e.g. in recent times *flared*, *parka* or *hipsters*.

Fast Food: The burger bar
Pre-Intermediate

1
■ Introduce the topic of fast food by asking students if they like burgers and pizzas. Elicit from them the names of different kinds of burgers and pizzas, what they like in their burgers and what toppings they have on pizzas. Build up a list of ingredients on the board.
■ Allow 10 minutes for students to do exercise 1.
■ Check answers.

2
■ Ask students to work in pairs on exercise 2. Ask them to think carefully about the best answers – look at the prices as well as the descriptions. Allow 15 minutes.
■ Check answers

3
■ Ask students to do exercise 3 and then to discuss answers in small groups. Allow 10-15 minutes.

Answers
1 1 tomato ketchup; 2 mayonnaise; 3 garlic sauce; 4 chilli sauce; 5 mustard; 6 lettuce; 7 tomatoes; 8 onions; 9 mushrooms; 10 pineapples; 11 cheese
2 2 Original; 3 Mushroom Supreme; 4 All Star; 5 Chilliburger; 6 Hawaiian; 7 Garlicburger; 8 Mexican
3 Students' own answers.

Fast Food: The pizza restaurant
Intermediate

1 & 2
■ Ask students to work in pairs on exercise 1. Allow 10 minutes.
■ Check answers.
■ Allow 15 minutes for exercise 2.
■ Check answers.

3
■ The listening part will take about 30 minutes.
■ Play recording through for general comprehension before attempting exercise 3. Check for level with some general questions: How many people did you hear? Did they all order pizzas? How many ordered desserts? etc.
■ Play recording again for students to find the answers to exercise 3. You may have to play it more than once to allow for writing time. Students could tick off the items on the menu in the worksheet.
■ Check answers.

4
■ You will probably need to hand out copies of the tapescript for students to do exercise 4.
■ Check answers.
■ Finish by playing the recording again and asking students to repeat.
■ Students can then read the dialogue in small groups.

Teacher's notes

Answers

1 1 c; 2 g; 3 a; 4 f; 5 h; 6 e; 7 j; 8 b; 9 d; 10 i
2 a garlic mushrooms; b side salad; c chocolate fudge cake; d ice cream; e garlic bread; f milkshake; g onion rings; h apple pie and cream; i cola; j fries
3 Pizzas: 1 x Chef's Special + fries, 1 x Margherita + fries, 1 x Vegetarian + side salad, 1 x Garlic treat + garlic bread + onion rings, 1 x Hot 'n' Spicy + side salad
   Drinks: 1 x banana milkshake, 1 x strawberry milkshake, 2 x cokes, 1 x glass of water
   Desserts: 1 x chocolate fudge cake
4 Laura: £5.90 + £1.50 + £1.50 = £8.90
   Daniel: £6.45 + £1.00 + £0.75 + £2.00 = £10.20
   Rachael: £5.90 + £1.50 + £1.50 = £8.90
   Abbie: £5.80 + £1.20 + £1.25 = £8.25
   Jamie: £4.70 + £1.00 + £0.75 = £6.45
   Total bill: £42.70

Tapescript

Daniel: I'm really starving. I'm going to have the Chef's Special.
Jamie: Yeah, me too!
Laura: Don't be stupid, Jamie – you haven't got enough money.
Jamie: Yes, I have. Oh, right, maybe not.
Laura: You'll have to have a Margherita.
Jamie: Oh, OK then, but I'll have some fries with it!
Rachael: Yes, me too!
Daniel: Yes, fries for me too.
Laura: I'll have the vegetarian pizza and a side salad, please. What about you, Abbie?
Abbie: The Garlic Treat for me ... with garlic bread and onion rings, please.
Daniel: Ugh! How can you eat all that garlic?
Abbie: I just love it.
Rachael: ... and I'll have the 'Hot 'n' Spicy' – I don't think I'll have fries with that so can you change it to a side salad? Oh yes, and a banana milkshake.
Laura: Mmm. I'll have a strawberry one.
Daniel: A coke for me, please
Jamie: Me too!
Daniel: Jamie, you're pathetic – you always copy me!
Jamie: Well, you obviously have very good taste!
Abbie: Can I just have a glass of water please?
Rachael: ... all that garlic!
Daniel: I'm going to have chocolate fudge cake afterwards.
Laura: Oh Daniel, you'll be sick!
Jamie: Well don't be sick over me.
Abbie: I don't think I'll want anything else.
Rachael: Nor me.
Jamie: No way.
Abbie: I couldn't.
Laura: So it's just Daniel's fudge cake. Daniel, you're such a pig!

1 & 2

■ The main point of this part is to introduce the subject of film ratings and advertisements. Elicit from the students the rating system in their country, and how they decide which film to go and see.
■ Talk about ticket prices in the cinema and how they can get any discounts on the full price.
■ Allow 15-20 minutes for the students to read the advertisement and do the two exercises.
■ Check answers.

Answers

1 15 No-one under the age of 15 is allowed to see this film.
   12 No children under the age of 12 can see this film.
   12A Children under the age of 12 can only see this film if they are accompanied by an adult.
   PG This film may not be suitable for a child under the age of 12. It is for the parents to decide if they want their child to see this film, so it depends on parental guidance.
   U   Anyone can go to see this film, it has a universal certificate.
2 1 No, not on Wednesday; 2 2 hours 20 minutes – till 6.00; 3 At 5.20; 4 At 9.10; 5 £11.80; 6 £11.80; 7 £11.95; 8 £1.50

Cultural References

■ OAP: Old Age Pensioner. In Britain, a man of 65 and over, or a woman of 60 or over, gets a state pension and can get a reduction on the price of a cinema ticket

1

■ Introduce the topic by asking the students to discuss in pairs the latest films they have seen and what kinds of films they like and don't like. Build up a list of the different kinds of films – thriller, romance – etc. and associated vocabulary – actor, director, – etc.
■ Ask students to read the reviews, ignoring the gaps, with the help of a dictionary.
■ Allow students 15 minutes to do exercise 1 in pairs.
■ Check answers.

2 & 3

■ Allow students 10 minutes to do exercises 2 and 3.
■ Check answers.
■ Ask students if they have seen any of the films and if they agree with the reviews.

Answers

1 1 Spy Kids 2; 2 My Big Fat Greek Wedding, Swimfan; 3 Signs, Insomnia; 4 Insomnia; 5 My Big Fat Greek Wedding; 6 Spy Kids 2; 7 Signs;

Teacher's notes

8 Swimfan; 9 Probably Spy Kids 2.; 10 Students' own answers
2 2 ending; 3 script; 4 teen movie; 5 plot; 6 cast; 7 character; 8 leading role; 9 acting; 10 comedy; 11 believable; 12 performance; 13 fun; 14 special effects; 15 direction; 16 family movie; 17 entertaining; 18 adventure
3 2 plot; 3 believable; 4 thriller; 5 acting; 6 character; 7 direction; 8 fun; 9 adventure; 10 special effects; 11 family movie; 12 comedy; 13 cast; 14 script; 15 lead role; 16 teen movie; 17 entertaining; 18 ending

Cultural References

A crop circle (Signs): This phenomenon was first seen in Britain about 20 years ago. In the summer, when the fields of corn or other cereals are nearly ready to cut, a strange pattern of circles occasionally appears in the field. No-one knows how these are made, though most people think they are man-made.

Cinema: Film reviews 2
Upper Intermediate

1
■ Ask students to work in pairs to discuss their favourite movies of all time. Ask them to think about why they really enjoyed them. Also, ask them to think about what the worst films were and why.
■ Allow 10 minutes to do the first exercise.
■ Check answers.

2 & 3
■ Now ask them to write their own review in 10 minutes. It should be quite short but contain all the important information.
■ Ask students to work in small groups to complete their lists of the top 5 films and discuss their choices.
■ Finish with a class vote to find the favourite film in the class.

Answers
1 1 Legally Blonde, Cruel intentions; 2 Clueless, Cruel Intentions, Romeo and Juliet; 3 Romeo and Juliet, Crossroads; 4 Clueless, Romeo and Juliet; 5 Clueless; 6 Romeo and Juliet
2,3 Students' own answers

Television: Programmes and listings
Intermediate

1
■ Elicit from students the kinds of TV programmes they watch. See if they know the names of these kinds of programmes in English.
■ Allow 15 minutes for students to do exercise 1.
■ Check answers.

2 & 3
■ Ask students to read the programme descriptions, using a dictionary if necessary. Allow 15 minutes to do exercise 2.
■ Check answers.
■ Finish by asking students to do exercise 3. Allow 10 minutes.

4
■ Refer students to the model descriptions of programmes in Part 1.
■ Elicit an example on the board for the first description – Parkinson.
■ Students can work individually or in pairs to write the descriptions. Allow 20 minutes.

5
■ Students write answers to the three questions about their favourite TV programmes on a piece of paper. Allow 5 minutes.
■ In small groups, students put their papers in, for example, a hat, and draw them out one by one. One student reads the paper and the other students must guess who they think wrote it.

6
■ Students work in pairs to prepare their TV evening. To make sure they have a variety of programmes in their plans, remind them of the possibilities from exercise 1. Allow 15 minutes to do the task.
■ Pairs can then compare their plans in small groups.

Answers
1 1 documentary; 2 soap; 3 sitcom; 4 cartoon; 5 talkshow; 6 drama; 7 news; 8 wildlife; 9 comedy; 10 gameshow; 11 sports
2 2 The Goal Rush – sports: scores, match, Premiership; 3 Merseybeat – drama: cops, death; 4 Play your Cards Right – gameshow: contestants, compete, prize; 5 Tonight with Trevor McDonald – news: Tonight, interviews, headlines; 6 Holby city – (hospital) drama: patient, urgent medical treatment, police, doctors, nurses, survive, crisis; 7 Live with… Chris Moyles – talkshow: host, chats; 8 Great Britons – documentary: (the names of people), true story; 9 The Life of Mammals – wildlife (documentary): mammals, animals, wildlife; 10 Coronation Street – soap: events, last Friday, daughter, problems, family; 11 Looney Toons – cartoon: Toons, crazy characters, amazing adventures

Teacher's notes

3 1 5, channels; 2 episode; 3 contestants, compete; 4 host, chats; 5 crisis, hospital

Cultural References

In Britain, normal, terrestrial TV has 5 channels: BBC1, BBC2, ITV, Channel 4, Channel 5. Everyone with a TV has these channels, except about 20% of the country who cannot receive Channel 5. In addition, there are many satellite and cable channels. Everyone who has a TV in Britain must pay for a licence. At present, this costs £112 per year. The money for this licence pays for the BBC TV and radio, which is a public service and has no advertising. The other channels are 'commercial' and are paid for by advertisements.

Soaps: These stories about families, neighbours and friends are the most popular TV programmes in Britain. They are normally half-hour programmes shown 3 or 4 times a week. The most famous ones are *Coronation Street*, about the lives of a group of people from Weatherfield, near Manchester in the North of England, and *Eastenders*, about people in the East End of London. *Coronation Street* has been running for more than 40 years. The name *soap* comes from the nickname *soap opera*, because the programmes used to be sponsored by companies producing and advertising soap products for washing clothes.

Computer Games: Reviews
Intermediate/Upper Intermediate

1

■ Discuss students' experience of computer games. Which games do you think are educational as well as fun? What exactly can you learn from them (knowledge; skills, etc.)? What are some typical activities you do in computer games?

■ Hand out the worksheet. Students read the descriptions of the 9 computer games, with dictionaries if necessary. Answer questions on specific vocabulary items (see Language Notes below).

■ In pairs or small groups, students discuss which game they would each choose and why.

■ Students briefly discuss and compare their choices in the whole group.

2

■ This activity practises more detailed comprehension of the texts. Give student 15 minutes for this matching activity before checking answers.

3

■ Give students 5 minutes to do this vocabulary recognition exercise.

■ Check answers.

Answers

1 Derek: Starry Night Backyard
Polly: Traitors' Gate
Charlie: Who Wants To Be A Millionaire 2
Stephen: Amerzone

Beth: Mystery of the Druids
Liam: Robot Arena
Hannah: Sim Triple Pack
Sam: Grand Prix 4

2 2 eclipse; 3 face up to; 4 herd, pride; 5 amateur; 6 tunes; 7 tackle; 8 Scotland Yard; 9 intrigued

Language Notes and Cultural References

■ *bugged replica jewels* means that the (fake) replacement jewels will have a miniaturised recording device hidden in them to bug (i.e. record) the thieves

■ *Tower of London:* A historic building near the river Thames. Built in the 11th century by William the Conqueror, it has been at various times a palace, a prison, a royal treasury (the crown jewels of the British monarchy are still kept there), and one of London's most popular tourist attractions.

■ *click on any body:* here *body* means 'heavenly body' i.e. star, planet, moon, etc.

■ *Watch the sparks fly:* Colliding metal objects can literally cause sparks (tiny bright pieces of burning material) to fly, but this expression is also idiomatic, meaning to settle a conflict in an excited, angry way.

■ Chris Tarrant is the well-known presenter of the British (and original) version of this programme.

■ Stonehenge is a prehistoric monument in southern England, over 4000 years old, consisting of a massive circle of standing stones. It is believed to have been used by pagan priests called druids for religious rituals and astronomical calculations.

Books: At the library
Intermediate

1

■ Students match the items by writing book titles underneath the appropriate category.

■ Check answers. Analyse what key words indicate the category the book belongs to. For example: *Greatest…* is associated with being famous; *Desserts* are something to eat so clearly connected with food; *Pottery* is the craft or activity of making objects out of clay, so belongs to the arts and crafts category, and so on.

2

■ Point out to students that for this task it is not necessary to understand all the elements in the texts. It is enough to identify topic words and phrases.

■ Check answers.

Answers

1 Reference: The Oxford Children's Encyclopaedia, Guinness Book of Answers
Traditional Tales, Myths and Legends: British Folk Tales, God and Heroes from Viking Mythology, The Wanderings of Odysseus
Arts and Crafts: Life Drawing, An Introduction to Pottery
Animals: The Snake Book, Naturewatch: Bears and Pandas

Teacher's notes

Sports: Rough Water Canoeing, Young Gymnast
Famous People: 100 Greatest Women, J.K.
Rowling: The Wizard behind Harry Potter;
Religions: Lives of the Saints, Sikhism
Politics and Society: What happens in Parliament, United Nations
Food and Drink: Cool Desserts, Confident Cooking
General Fiction: Madame Doubtfire, Dr Jekyll and Mr Hyde;
Computers: A Guide to Programming, Teach yourself e-commerce

2 British Folk Tales: Once upon a time …; 'If only we had even one child …'; 'Yes,' said his wife …
Naturewatch: Bears and Pandas: A rare and closely protected animal …; Their thick woolly coat is black …; Bamboo constitutes most of their diet …
Cool Desserts: Beat the egg whites …; Remove the blackcurrant mixture …; Return to the container …

Books: Blurbs
Intermediate/Upper Intermediate
1 - 4

■ The titles presented in this activity are all recently published by Scholastic. Students may, however, prefer to start with abridged and graded stories. Handling books is a first step in breaking down resistance to reading. If you have access to graded readers, bring a selection to class for a 'browsing' session. Working alone, or in groups, students can prepare short oral reports on a title they have looked at, based on the blurb and book jacket design or read one page of a book, make a note of how many words they did not understand, and thus gauge their own level of reading.

■ Discuss students' tastes in reading. Ask who has read any fiction in the last three months? (L1 or L2). Ask for examples of some of the genres of popular fiction (e.g.: crime and detection; fantasy; romance; classic literature).

■ Read the 5 blurbs. Students should not be too concerned at this stage about the meanings of difficult words. The exercises will guide them to an understanding of the essential points, and exercise 4 will pick up some of the unfamiliar vocabulary.

■ Give students 15-20 minutes to do exercises 1-4.

5

■ This exercise can also be a discussion phase, practising the language of likes, dislikes, preferences, etc.
I'm not really into... I (don't) really like... I'm (not so) keen on...

6

■ Creative writing. It would help if students could read further examples of book jacket blurbs, for example those on graded readers. Remind them

that the purpose of a blurb is not just to provide information, but also to attract the potential reader.

■ If students need more guidance, the following questions on the illustration may help:
Where is this scene taking place?
Do the young man and woman know each other?
Are they interested in each other? (How do you know?)
Describe the two dogs.
What do you think the dogs are going to do?
What about the two young people?
How will the story develop?

Answers
1 1 Footloose; 2 The Haunting of Alaizabel Cray; 3 Plex; 4 My Funny Valentine; 5 Blood Sinister
2 1 Shauna; 2 Ellen Forrest; 3 the wych kin; 4 Kelly; 5 Mr Multiplex; 6 Alaizabel Cray
3 1 Blood Sinister; 2 My Funny Valentine; 3 Footloose; 4 The Haunting of Alaizabel Cray; 5 Plex
4 1 d; 2 c; 3 e; 4 a; 5 b

Sport: Vocabulary
Intermediate
1

■ Introduce the topic by talking about sports. Ask the students which sports they play and enjoy watching. Students could discuss this in pairs or small groups for 10 minutes and then teacher build a list on the board of vocabulary connected with sports and equipment.

■ Allow 15-20 minutes for students to do wordsearch and associated exercise.

■ Check answers.

2

■ Before beginning exercise 2, check students' knowledge of the difference between commonly used verbs like *play, win, beat, lose, score*, etc.

■ Allow 10 minutes for the exercise.

■ Check answers.

Answers
1 2 racket; 3 club; 4 bat; 5 trainers; 6 net; 7 helmet; 8 gloves; 9 boots
2 1 won, League; 2 played, at, lost, games; 3 team, league, win, play, at; 4 play, win; 5 team, beating, teams; 6 match, scored, goals

Teacher's notes

Sport: Sports reports
Upper Intermediate

1
- Check students' knowledge of words associated with different sports by eliciting words like *try, draw, hole*.
- Allow 10 minutes for students to do the matching exercise. Ask them to pick out the words which gave them the clues and check in dictionaries if necessary.
- Check answers.

2
- Introduce the topic of football. Ask students which teams they support and why. Ask students what they know about football in England. See how many players and teams they can name.
- Ask students to read the match summaries and to do the exercise. Allow 15 minutes.
- Check answers.

Answers
1 1 h; 2 b; 3 e; 4 l; 5 i; 6 k; 7 g; 8 c; 9 f; 10 a; 11 j; 12 d
2 2 West Ham; 3 No (uninspiring); 4 Five; 5 No (goal drought); 6 The number of matches the club have won one after another at home in the league.; 7 The first half; 8 No (disputed); 9 None.

Sport: League table
Upper Intermediate

1
- Elicit from students their knowledge of the leagues in their own country. Ask them to explain how it works – what the different columns mean, how the points system is counted, etc.
- Ask them to look at the extracts from the Premiership. Before they start, make sure students have looked at the key and understand how the tables work. Allow 15 minutes for them to complete the exercise. Students can work in pairs or in small groups.
- Check answers.
- To finish, students could work in small groups to make up their own tables and then ask and answer questions from other students about their tables.

Answers

1		P		HOME						AWAY					GD	Pts
			W	D	L	F	A		W	D	L	F	A		
1	Arsenal	7	4	0	0	11	4		1	2	0	6	3	10	17
2	Liverpool	7	2	2	0	9	4		2	1	0	6	4	7	15
3	ManUtd	7	3	0	0	6	3		1	1	2	5	6	2	13
4	Leeds	6	2	0	1	4	1		2	0	1	6	3	6	12
5	Chelsea	6	1	2	0	6	3		2	1	0	7	5	5	12
17	Man City	6	1	0	2	4	5		1	0	2	3	6	-4	6
18	Aston Villa	7	1	3	0	2	1		0	0	3	1	6	4	6
19	Bolton	7	0	1	2	1	5		1	1	2	1	5	-8	5
20	West Ham	6	0	2	2	2	5		0	0	2	2	7	-8	2

3 7; 4 7; 5 Arsenal, Liverpool, Chelsea; 7 12; 8 1; 9 4; 10 3

Cultural References
The premiership is the top football league in England and has twenty teams. Each season, the bottom three teams are relegated and the top teams from the next division (the first division) are promoted.

Songs: Lyrics
Intermediate

1-11
- Before asking students to start looking at the songs, ask them what they know about Alicia Keys and Daniel Bedingfield. Also discuss their favourite singers, why they like them and the English songs they know.
- It's best for students to work through the exercises from start to finish. Students should preferably work in small groups because the tasks are quite difficult. Make it a competition to see which team can finish first. Allow 30-40 minutes.
- If students know the songs, they can try reading or singing the lyrics when fully corrected.

Answers
Song A - Girlfriend
Baby, silly for me to feel this way
about you and her,
Cos' I know she's been such a good friend
I know she has helped you through.

Talkin late on the phone
Every night you've been callin
Private moments alone
And your heart soon be fallin
And I know she's a friend
But I can't shake the feeling
That I could be losing your heart.

Chorus
I think I'm jealous of your girlfriend
Although she's just a girl that is your friend
I think I'm jealous of your girlfriend
She shares a special part of you

You said that she's done well to see
How deep you're in love with me
And intentions were not to get in between
But I see possibilities

And you say that you feel
I'm the best thing in your life
And I know it's real, see it in your eyes
There's no reason for me, to even feel this way
I know you just enjoy her company

(Chorus)

Teacher's notes

(Alicia Keys, Jermaine Dupri, Joshua Thompson)
Published by Lello Music Publishing/EMI Music
Publishing (ASCAP)

Song B – If You're Not the One

If you're not the one then why does my soul feel
glad today?
If you're not the one then why does my hand fit
yours this way?
If you are not mine then why does your heart
return my call?
If you are not mine would I have the strength to
stand at all?
I never know what the future brings
but I know you are here with me now.
We'll make it through and I hope
You are the one I share my life with

Chorus

I don't want to run away but I can't
take it I don't understand
If I'm not made for you then why
does my heart tell me that I am?
Is there any way that I can stay in your arms?

If I don't need you then why am I crying on my bed?
If I don't need you then why does your name
resound in my head?
If you're not for me then why does this distance
maim my life?
If you're not for me then why do I dream of you as
my wife?

I don't know why you're so far away
But I know that this much is true
We'll make it through and I hope
You are the one I share my life with
And I wish that you could be the one I die with
And I'm praying you're the one I build my home
with
I hope I love you all my life

(Chorus)

Cos I miss you
Body and soul so strong that
it takes my breath away
And I breathe you into my heart
and pray for the strength to stand today.
Cos I love you
Whether it's wrong or right and
though I can't be with you tonight
And though my heart is by your side.

(Chorus)

(Daniel Bedingfield)
Published by Sony/ATV Music Publishing UK Ltd on
Polydor records

FOR REAL! © MARY GLASGOW MAGAZINES, AN IMPRINT OF SCHOLASTIC INC.

Museum: At the museum
Pre-Intermediate/Intermediate

1

■ Give students a few minutes to study the icons
before doing the matching activity. With the less
obvious examples, discuss what the service is, e.g.
Who needs Babycare? What for? What is
provided?
When is First Aid needed? What are museum
staff trained to do?

2

■ Play recording. Tell students that they won't
have to understand every word of the listening
in order to do the task.
■ Check answers.
■ You could then play the recording again and ask
students to answer these questions:
   1 Describe, in one sentence, the object that the
   young man has lost.
   2 What are the man and woman doing?
   What does the woman decide to do next?
   The woman says, 'I'll catch you up.' What does
   she mean?
   3 You are the waiter. Write down on your order
   pad what the boy and girl are going to have.
   4 What is the woman collecting? Describe the
   items she wants.
   5 What has happened to the elderly gentleman?
   6 What does the Attendant suggest for the
   schoolchildren?
   Where do the lectures and films take place?
   7 What does the young man buy?

3

■ Encourage students to do this scanning exercise
quickly, using key words in the texts as clues.
■ Students compare answers in pairs before class
feedback.

Answers

1 2 Toilets; 3 Babycare; 4 Ticket desk; 5 Disabled
toilet; 6 Lost property; 7 Restaurant; 8 Audio
tour; 9 First Aid; 10 Cloakroom; 11 Shop; 12 Café
2 1 Lost property; 2 Babycare; 3 Café; 4 Cloakroom;
5 First Aid; 6 Information; 7 Shop
3 2 Tower Bridge Experience; 3 Madame Tussaud's
Waxworks; 4 Sherlock Holmes Museum;
5 National Maritime Museum; 6 Imperial War
Museum; 7 London Dungeon; 8 Shakespeare's
Globe Exhibition & Theatre; 9 Victoria & Albert
Museum; 10 Science Museum

Tapescript

1 A: *Excuse me. I've lost a brown rucksack. I*
wonder if it's been handed in.
B: *When did you lose it?*
A: *About half an hour ago, I think. I was in the*
Chase Manhattan gallery, rooms 26 and 27.
B: *Brown, did you say?*
A: *Yes, light brown. It's got a logo on the front*
of a swallow. And there are some books in it

Teacher's notes

and a pullover.

B: Just a minute. I'll have a look.

2 A: Have you got the clean nappy?

B: Yes, here it is.

A: Thanks. Here's the dirty one — could you dispose of it?

B: OK. Where's the bin? Ah, here it is.

A: I think I might give him a feed while we're in here.

B: All right. Shall I stay?

A: No, you go ahead. I'll catch you up.

B: OK. I'll take the bags.

3 A: What are you going to have?

B: I'll have a coke. What about you?

A: I'm not sure. Do you fancy something to eat?

B: Wouldn't mind. But I don't want much.

A: They only have sandwiches, cakes, crisps, that sort of thing.

B: I think I might have one of these chocolate chip muffins.

A: OK. I'll have a tuna and mayonnaise sandwich. And a cappuccino.

4 A: Here's my ticket.

B: Right. Just a moment, please. Here you are.

A: No, sorry, this isn't my coat.

B: Oh.

A: And that's not my scarf, either. Mine is a long grey raincoat. With silver buttons.

B: Right. I'll have another look.

5 A: Oh…could you help please — an elderly gentleman has just fallen down the stairs.

B: I'll come right away.

6 A: Excuse me, I'd like to come here again, next week, with a party of school children. Could you tell me if there are any tours or events for groups of young people during the week?

B: Well, there's a programme of lectures films and videos which take place during term time, in rooms under the main museum concourse. Also, you might be interested in the Ford Centre for Young Visitors, which has special lunchrooms, cloakrooms and other facilities for school groups.

A: Oh, that sounds good…

7 A: Excuse me. How much is this poster here?

B: One moment. Jane, how much is the poster of the Raphael drawing?

C: It's £15.

A: OK I'll have it. And do you have any postcards of the Aztec god Tezcatlipoca?

B: No, I'm afraid we've sold out for the moment.

A: OK. That's all then.

C: That'll be £15 please.

Visitor Attractions: Hampton Court & Leeds Castle
Intermediate

1

■ Use a map of Britain to point out the location of Hampton Court, to the South West of London, and Leeds Castle, in Kent (not in Leeds!).

■ Ask students if they know the names of any of the Kings and Queens of England. In particular do they know any facts about King Henry VIII?

■ Complete the vocabulary exercise 1, which will help to pre-teach some of the vocabulary required for the listening activity.

■ Check answers.

2

■ Before listening, give students 2 minutes to look at the table of attractions.

■ Play audio recording. Students tick the attractions found in each place (some are to be found in both places).

■ Discuss answers with the class.

■ Play recording again to check and confirm answers.

■ Extension: Discussion or writing.

Answers

1 1 dog collar; 2 vine; 3 maze; 4 aviary; 5 costume; 6 moat; 7 wander; 8 peacock

2

	Hampton Court	Leeds Castle
royal connections	✓	✓
built in the 11th century		✓
Henry VIII lived there	✓	✓
beautiful rooms you can visit	✓	
beautiful gardens	✓	✓
walks along the river	✓	
a maze	✓	
shops	✓	✓
places to eat and drink	✓	✓
Tudor kitchens	✓	
an aviary		✓
a very old vine	✓	
a golf course		✓
an unusual museum		✓
lakes and a moat		✓
tours with guides in costume	✓	
a fine collection of paintings	✓	
a Shakespeare play in the summer		✓

Tapescript

Hampton Court is near Richmond in south west London. It's easy to get to from the centre of the city: you can catch a train from Waterloo station or even take a boat down the river Thames from Westminster. Hampton court has been home to many of Britain's famous kings and queens including Henry VIII, Charles I, and William and Mary. You should see the lavishly decorated state apartments and the Great Hall with its original tapestries. The palace also boasts one of the finest collections of Renaissance paintings in Europe. One of the highlights of any tour is the vast Tudor kitchens. In the time of Henry VIII up to 1200 people a day were fed from these kitchens. Today

Teacher's notes

they are laid out as if a feast was being prepared, with a roaring log fire and dishes that include roast peacock and desserts decorated with real gold. If you want the historical background to Hampton Court, there are expert guides wearing period costumes ready to give you a guided tour.

The formal gardens are a great feature too: you can walk through them to the River Thames, or you can get lost in the famous maze.

The Palace is also home to one of the oldest vines in the world, which still produces about 300 kg. of grapes a year.

If you want something to eat or drink you can choose from the Tiltyard tearooms or the Privy Kitchen Coffee Shop. The palace shops offer a wide range of gifts and souvenirs.

Leeds Castle is in Kent in the south-east corner of England. You can get a National Express coach there or you can travel by train from Victoria station on an "all-in-one" ticket which includes admission to the castle.

Leeds was built just after the Norman Conquest of 1066 AD and many kings and queens including Henry VIII used it as a residence. It's in a lovely setting, surrounded by lakes and a moat. There are woods for the visitor to wander through, and formal gardens with a maze to get lost in. Children will enjoy the Secret Grotto with its underground caves. And if you like bird spotting you'll find plenty of wildfowl: including the famous black swans on the castle lakes. There's an aviary, too, with more than a hundred species of birds.

Although at present there are no tours of the interior of the castle, there's plenty to see and do around it. You can visit the fascinating Museum of Dog Collars — the only one of its kind in Britain; there are shops and restaurants, and, if you are so inclined, there's a nine hole golf course where you can play a round amidst some of the loveliest scenery in the country.

There are special events at the castle all the year round. These include performances of Shakespeare's Romeo and Juliet on the Pavilion lawn in early June, and a grand fireworks spectacular during the first week of November.

Language Notes and Cultural References

The Tudor dynasty of Kings and Queens began in 1485 with Henry VII and ended with the death of Queen Elizabeth I in 1603.

The Norman Conquest of 1066 was the invasion of England by the Norman (French) King, William I. He defeated the English King, Harold, at the Battle of Hastings. After this, England was ruled by a French-speaking court, with far-reaching consequences for political organisation, social life and the development of the English language.

tapestries: large pieces of cloth hung on walls for decoration. They have designs or pictures sewn on them with coloured thread.

roaring log fire: an open fire of large pieces of wood, burning noisily.

Mobile Phones: Text messages
Intermediate

1
- Introduce the topic of mobile phones and texting. Ask students how many have mobile phones, how they use them, how they pay for them, the advantages and disadvantages, etc. Elicit from students the subject of texting and some of the abbreviations they use in their own language when sending messages.
- Go through the pronunciation of the English alphabet. Make sure the students know how to pronounce the letters. Go through the numbers 1- 10. Make sure the students know how to pronounce the numbers.
- Ask students to do exercise 1. Allow 10-15 minutes.
- Check answers. Go through pronunciation of the items.

2 & 3
- Allow 10-15 minutes for exercise 2.
- Check answers. Go through pronunciation of the items.
- Students do exercise 3. Allow 15-20 minutes.
- Check answers. Go through pronunciation of the items.

4
- Ask students to do the dialogue exercise. This may be best in pairs.
- Check answers. Students could then practise reading the dialogues together in pairs.

Answers
1 1 at; 2 be; 3 see; 4 got to go; 5 and; 6 Are; 7 t-shirt; 8 you; 9 Why
2 1 (8) late; 2 (8) great; 3 (2) tomorrow; 4 (8) skating; 5 (2) tonight; 6 (1) someone; 7 (8) mate; 8 (8) date
3 2 i; 3 l; 4 k; 5 g; 6 b; 7 a; 8 h; 9 j; 10 f; 11 n; 12 e; 13 c; 14 o; 15 m
4 Hello, how are you? What are you doing today? Do you want to meet at 11 o'clock? Text back. OK. What do you want to do? What are you going to wear?
Meet in town and shop. I'm going to wear jeans and a t-shirt.

Cultural References
Mate: Young people use mate to talk about a good friend. Traditionally, a mate is the person you marry or have children with. It is also used for someone who helps you in your job, or shares a part of your life – *workmate, classmate, flatmate*, etc.

Teacher's notes

Mobile Phones: Conversations
Pre-Intermediate/Intermediate

1 & 2
- Give students 10 minutes to do the matching exercise.
- Check answers. Judy is the one with no speaking partner; she has to leave a recorded message.

3
- Students read some of the text more intensively to answer these questions.
- Students can compare answers in pairs before class feedback.
- Get students to practise the conversations in pairs. Rotate pairs and repeat until everyone can reproduce at least 3 of the conversations from memory.
- Extension. In pairs students write a two-line mobile phone exchange in which they arrange to meet / talk about what they are doing / ask for something / discuss their plans for the evening. They cut the conversation into two strips. Collect the two halves of each conversation, shuffle and redistribute, one to each student. Students read out their half dialogues and try to find their 'other halves'.

Answers
1,2 The speaking partners are: Martin and Diane; Val and Richard; Megan and Kirsten; Rita and Eleanor; Sean and Paul; Joe and Janet; Neil and Carol; Matthew and Sid; Judy has no partner
2 1 Sean; 2 Richard; 3 Eleanor; 4 Sid; 5 Megan; 6 Diane; 7 Janet; 8 Judy; 9 Neil

What To Say: Conversations
Pre-Intermediate/Intermediate

1
- Working individually or in pairs, students look at pictures 1-12, read the second half of each conversational exchange and try to guess what the first speaker is saying.
- Discuss suggested answers as a class. Write a few plausible suggestions on the board. Ask which exchanges seem to be requests for information (e.g. no. 6), and which ones requests for action (e.g. no. 9).
- Play recording. Students listen but do not write.
- Students then try to recall any sentences they can from the recording and write them in rough on a separate piece of paper.
- Play recording again, stopping as often as necessary. Students write remaining answers, still in rough.
- Check answers.
- Play recording for 3rd time. Students transcribe correct sentences from rough paper to the activity sheet.

2
- Students practise all the dialogues in pairs.

3
- Play the recording again. This time students have to remember the replies, without looking at their completed activity sheet.

Answers
(see tapescript below)

Tapescript
1 A: Do you know where Broadmarsh Road is, please?
  B: Sorry, I can't help you. I'm a stranger here myself.
2 A: Have you seen a little black dog anywhere?
  B: No, I haven't, but I'll look out for it.
3 A: I've got my final examinations next week.
  B: Good luck! I'll be thinking of you.
4 A: Can I try these jeans on, please?
  B: Yes, sure. The fitting rooms are at the back of the store.
5 A: Do you mind if I open the window?
  B: No, go ahead.
6 A: Whereabouts in London do you live?
  B: In Notting Hill. It's in the west of the city.
7 A: Could you lend me £5 until we get back home?
  B: No problem. You can borrow ten if you want.
8 A: Could I use the toilet, please?
  B: Yes, of course. It's at the top of the stairs, first door on the left.
9 A: Can you help? I've cut my finger.
  B: Oh dear. Hang on, I'll get a plaster.
10 A: Is there any food you don't like?
  B: Well, I'm not too keen on raw tomatoes.
11 A: Guido – come and join us!
  B: I'd like to, but I'm on my way to meet someone.
12 A: How are you getting on in your new school?
  B: Fine. I really like it.

Greetings Cards: Messages
Intermediate

1
- With students, look at the list of occasions for sending greetings in Britain. Compare with customs in the students' own country.
- Discuss what is marked or celebrated in each case, and why. (see Cultural References below)
- Give students 5 minutes for the matching activity. Do not check their answers yet.

2
- Give students 10 minutes for this word ordering and matching activity.
- Students can compare their answers to exercises 1 and 2 in pairs before class feedback.

Teacher's notes

3

■ Explain that it is customary to add a short personal message inside a greetings card.

■ Class discussion: It's now easy to send pictures and messages to people (including commercial greetings cards) using electronic communications such as mobile phones, the internet, etc. Does this mean traditional greetings cards will disappear? Give reasons for and against sending traditional cards.

Answers

1,2 Card 2: Christmas, b – Merry Christmas and a happy new year
Card 3: getting married, a – Wishing you both good luck and happiness in the future
Card 4: a birthday, g – Many happy returns of the day
Card 5: Valentine's Day, e – With love from a secret admirer
Card 6: Mother's Day, f – To the best mum in the world
Card 7: a wedding anniversary, j – Best wishes on your silver anniversary
Card 8: to thank someone, i – Thanks a lot for the generous gift
Card 9: moving to a new home, c – Good luck in your new home
Card 10: the birth of a baby, d – Congratulations on the birth of your baby daughter
3 2 Card 3; 3 Card 10; 4 Card 5; 5 Card 1; 6 Card 9; 7 Card 4; 8 Card 8; 9 Card 7; 10 Card 2

Language Notes and Cultural References

■ *Tie the knot:* an idiomatic expression for 'get married'
■ *Little bundle of joy:* a new baby. A bundle is something wrapped up in cloth.
■ *Guess who?:* It is the custom not to sign a Valentine card with your own name, though some people like to give a cryptic clue as to the identity of the sender.
■ *From today…:* This is for an 18th birthday when all of these things become legally possible.
■ Mothering Sunday (or Mother's Day) is celebrated in Britain on the Sunday closest to 30 March. It's the special day when people remember their mothers with messages, visits or gifts. The purpose is to show how much we appreciate our mothers and all they have done for us, since being a mother is not an easy job, but it's very important!

Train: Announcements and signs
Intermediate

1

■ Introduce the topic by asking students if they enjoy train travel. Elicit the advantages / disadvantages of travelling by train. Ask if any students have travelled by train in other countries.
■ Look at the Cultural References below and ask students to compare these aspects with their own country.
■ Allow 15 minutes for students to do exercise 1. Allow dictionaries for support.
■ Check answers.

2

■ Explain to students that they will need to think about both meaning and grammatical forms to do this matching activity. Allow 10 minutes.

3

■ Before starting this exercise, make sure students understand the points from the Cultural References. Explain the importance of these warnings on British trains. Allow 10 minutes to do the exercise.
■ Ask students for their best-ever and worst-ever travelling by train stories – in pairs, then small groups and then in front of the whole class.

Answers

1 1 carriage/coach; 2 platform; 3 fare; 4 guard; 5 destination; 6 compartment; 7 ticket barrier
2 2 h; 3 j; 4 a; 5 g; 6 c; 7 i; 8 b; 9 e; 10 f
3 2 e; 3 a; 4 d; 5 c; 6 f

Cultural References

The live rail: In Britain most trains are electric. The live electric line is usually on the ground next to the other rails. You must not cross the line because you could be electrocuted.
Long trains: Trains are often quite long and different parts of the train may be going to different destinations. It's sometimes very important to read the notice and listen to the announcements to travel in the correct part of the train, usually either the front or rear four (six) coaches.
Tickets: Normally you must buy a ticket before you start your journey. This may not be possible on some smaller stations. Every train carries a guard who can issue tickets. If you haven't already got a ticket, buy one from the guard on the train.
Communication cord (chain): There is a communication cord in every carriage which will stop the train when pulled in an emergency. You must pay £50 if you pull this without reason.
Alight: To alight (alighted) means to get off a train or bus.

Teacher's notes

Bus: Vocabulary and fares
Intermediate

1
■ Introduce the topic by asking students about travelling by bus. Ask them if they use the bus, what they think about bus travel, if the buses are on time, crowded, friendly, etc. Try to elicit some of the vocabulary which they will meet in exercise 1.
■ Allow 10-15 minutes for exercise 1.
■ Check answers.

2
■ Introduce the topic of discount fares, travelcards, student cards etc. Ask the students if they have special cards. Talk about discounts for children (minimum ages), young people, students, unemployed people, Old Age Pensioners, etc.
■ Ask students to read the information about Saver fares and to ask about any difficult vocabulary.
■ Allow 15 minutes for this exercise.
■ Check answers.

Answers
1 1 catch; 2 queue, on; 3 off, stop; 4 missed; 5 fare; 6 conductor; 7 route; 8 journey; 9 Smoking
2 1 At all Post Offices and many newsagents; 2 £30; 3 No; 4 £1; 5 No; 6 £20; 7 10 pence; 8 Explorer Saver.

Cultural References
Conductors: In England, most buses only have a driver. Passengers get on at the front and pay the driver. Some buses in London have a conductor as well as a driver. With these buses, you usually get on at the back, take a seat, and the conductor comes round the bus to collect the fares.
Fares: In some places, there are flat fares. You can go anywhere for, for example, £1. But this isn't true everywhere. It's important to say where you are going and to have plenty of small change. Some bus drivers do not like changing £10 or £20 pound notes and others do not give change.

Bus: Timetables
Intermediate

1 & 2
■ Make sure the students are familiar with the idea of reading timetables. Ask them about timings and regularity of buses they use.
■ Allow 20 minutes for exercise 1.
■ Check answers.
■ Allow 10 minutes for exercise 2
■ Check answers

Answers
1

	a.m.	a.m.	a.m.	then at these minutes past each hour until		p.m.	p.m.	p.m.	p.m.	p.m.
Brighton Univ.	8.25	8.55	9.25	55	25	5.55	6.55	7.55	8.55	9.55
Lewes Road	8.28	8.58	9.28	58	28	5.58	6.58	7.58	8.58	9.58
Open Market	8.33	9.03	9.33	03	33	6.03	7.03	8.03	9.03	10.03
Old Steine	8.38	9.08	9.38	08	38	6.08	7.08	8.08	9.08	10.08
Brighton Stn	8.43	9.13	9.43	13	43	6.13	7.13	8.13	9.13	10.13

2 a.m. means the morning between 12 midnight and 12 midday, p.m. means the afternoon and night between 12 midday and 12 midnight.
3 18 minutes; 4 2.55 p.m.; 5 43 minutes; 6 9.55
2 1 7.03 – The Open Market; 2 2.08 – Old Steine; 3 11.03 – The Open Market; 4 4.13 – Brighton Station; 5 12.58 – Lewes Road; 6 3.28 – Lewes Road

Bus: Instructions
Pre-Intermediate

1
■ Play the recording once before students look at the exercise or the wordsearch. Tell students to listen carefully and try to remember the expressions.
■ Students can work together in pairs to complete the exercise and wordsearch. Allow 15-20 minutes.
■ Play recording again to check answers. Check wordsearch answers.

2
■ Allow 10 minutes for students to write their 3 good and bad things about bus travel.
■ Ask them to compare answers in small groups for 15 minutes. Each group should then agree upon its definitive list. Finish with a whole class discussion.

Answers and Tapescript
1 *Hold tight please!*
2 *Please do not speak to the driver.*
3 *Press to ring the bell.*
4 *Passengers are not allowed to stand beyond this point.*
5 *No change given.*
6 *Any more fares please!*
7 *Please extinguish all cigarettes.*
8 *Give up this seat to a disabled person.*

Teacher's notes

Airport: Announcements and notices
Pre-Intermediate

1
- Introduce the topic of flying and airports. Ask students if they like flying and airports. Ask them to share their experiences. Ask them to say what happens when they go to take a flight – the different procedures they have to go through. Elicit some of the vocabulary they are going to meet in the exercises.
- Allow 10 minutes for exercise 1.

2
- For the departures board exercise, play the recording once before they look at the exercise. Ask questions for general comprehension, e.g. *How many extracts did you hear? How many announcements? How many conversations? Can you name any of the places you heard?*
- Ask students to complete the information whilst listening to the recording a second time.
- Students check in pairs before listening to the recording a third time.
- Check answers.

3 & 4
- Ask students about airport security and changes since September 11th 2001.
- Ask students to look at the security notice and answer the 2 questions.
- Allow 10-15 minutes for students to match the items to the pictures. Allow dictionaries if appropriate.
- Finish with a general discussion on airport / aircraft security. *Should it be stricter? In what ways? Is it good to have armed guards on planes?* etc.

Answers
1   1 Boarding pass; 2 Check-in desk; 3 customs; 4 baggage claim; 5 excess baggage; 6 hand luggage; 7 luggage; 8 boarding gate; 9 aisle seat; 10 passenger

2
Flight	No.	Time	Destination	Information	Gate
EasyJet	7732	12.15	Brussels	Delayed - listen to announcements	-
Ryanair	325	12.25	Dublin	Final call	39
Swissair	414	12.30	Geneva	Final call	13
Alitalia	571	12.40	Rome	Final call	12
Lufthansa	3196	12.45	Prague	Now boarding	19
Iberian	268	13.05	Barcelona	Now boarding	42
SAS	108	13.30	Stockholm	Go to Airport Information	-
Air France	729	12.30	Marseilles	Delayed to 14.30	
Olympic Airways	4022	13.45	Athens	Delayed to 15.40	-

3   1 b; 2 b
4   1 hypodermic syringes; 2 razor blades; 3 toy or replica guns; 4 knives; 5 tools; 6 sports bats; 7 knitting needles; 8 catapults/slingshots; 9 cutlery; 10 darts; 11 scissors

Tapescript
1   *Iberian Airways flight 268 to Barcelona is now ready for boarding. Will all passengers for this flight proceed to gate 42.*

2   *This is the last call for passengers travelling to Rome on Alitalia flight 571, due to leave at 12.40. Will any remaining passengers please go immediately to gate 12 where the flight is now closing.*

3   *A: Excuse me. I have a ticket for the 12.30 flight to Marseilles. I was told to wait for announcements. Could you tell me what's happening?*
    B: Is that Air France?
    A: Yes, that's right, flight 729.
    B: I'm afraid the plane has been delayed because of technical problems. The new departure time is 14.30.
    A: Oh dear! Another two hours!

4   *This is the final call for passenger Jenkins travelling on Swissair flight number 414 to Geneva departing at 12.30. Will passenger Jenkins please go to gate 13 where the flight is ready to depart.*

5   *A: Oh no! Such terrible traffic and now I'm so late!.... erm, excuse me, has the 12.45 Lufthansa flight to Prague left yet?*
    B: What's the flight number?
    A: Oh, hang on a moment..... yes, here we are... it's 3196.
    B: Right, you're in luck. It's still boarding - at Gate 19. Check in quickly and you'll still make it.
    A: Thanks a million.

6   *This is an important announcement. Due to extreme weather conditions, Stockholm Airport has closed until tomorrow morning. Will all passengers on SAS flight 108, due to depart at 13.30, please report to the airport information desk. Thank you.*

7   *Olympic Airways regret to announce the delay of flight 4022 to Athens due to depart at 13.45. This flight is now scheduled to depart at 15.40.*

Airport: Check-in
Intermediate

1 & 2
- Ask students to read the incorrect dialogue before listening.
- Play recording once and allow time to write underlinings and corrections.
- Ask students to compare in pairs.
- Play recording again and afterwards ask students to confer again.
- Check answers in class.
- Play recording again and ask students to repeat. Pay attention to pronunciation, stress and intonation.
- Students read the conversation in pairs. Then switch roles. Then see if one half can remember

Teacher's notes

the words. then the other half. Finish by having two students try to recreate the dialogue in front of the whole class.

3

■ Ask students what information is contained on an airline ticket.

■ Allow 15-20 minutes for students to read the ticket and answer the 6 questions.

■ Check answers.

■ For homework students could write about their experiences of air travel.

Answers and Tapescript

1 Jane: Good morning.
Ground staff: Hello, can I see your ticket and passport, please? Is it just one <u>suitcase</u> you have?
Jane: Yes, and two <u>pieces</u> of hand luggage.
Ground staff: OK, can you just lift it onto the <u>scales</u>? Did you <u>pack</u> your suitcase yourself?
Jane: Yes.
Ground staff: Have you got any <u>electrical</u> or flammable items in your case?
Jane: No, I've got a walkman, razor and <u>mobile</u> phone with me here.
Ground staff: That's OK. Look at this list. Are you carrying any of the items in your hand luggage?
Jane: No, my <u>scissors</u> are in the case.
Ground staff: Good. Have you left your case <u>unattended</u> at any time since you packed it?
Jane: No.
Ground staff: OK, that's fine. Would you prefer a window seat or <u>aisle seat</u>?
Jane: I think a window seat, please.
Ground staff: Ok, here's your <u>boarding</u> pass with your seat number. It'll be Gate 25. If you go through <u>security</u> and passport control you can wait in the departure <u>lounge</u> ... or have a look at the shops while you're waiting. Make sure you look at the <u>screens</u> to see when your flight starts <u>boarding</u>. Have a good flight!
Jane: Thanks

3 1 a; 2 b; 3 c; 4 Saturday 13th April / Saturday 20th April; 5 Her passport; 6 She will have to put her gifts in her luggage and pay excess. She will also have to pay for 5 kilos excess on her suitcase.

1

■ Before handing out the worksheets, ask students to draw a simple outline map of Britain and/or the British Isles. If this is too difficult, draw one on the board for them to copy – a simple, geometric version of the one in this activity. Ask them to mark the following on the map:
England
Scotland
Wales
London
Edinburgh
the River Thames
Depending on their likely knowledge, you can also add Oxford, Cambridge, Manchester, Liverpool, Glasgow, Cardiff, etc.

■ Give out the worksheet. Students find the above places on the map. Practise geographical location, e.g. Where is Plymouth? It's on the south-west coast of England. Where is Aberdeen? It's on the north-east coast of Scotland. Where is Liverpool? It's in the north-west of England, on the River Mersey. etc.

■ Play audio recording. Students draw a line on the map to indicate the route taken by Tomas and Emilia.

■ Check answers.

2

■ In pairs students turn over the map and, working from memory, try to complete the quiz.

■ Students look at map and check their answers.

3

■ Give students 10 minutes to fill in the blanks by referring to the map.

■ Check answers.

■ Extension: refer back to the simple sketch map done at the beginning of the lesson. From memory mark the places and features mentioned in both exercises 2 and 3 on this first map. This can be done in pairs or by individuals coming out to the write on the board.

Answers

1 The line drawn on the map should follow this order:
London – Brighton – Stratford-Upon-Avon – Bath – Snowdonia (North Wales) – London – York – Edinburgh (Scotland) – Isle of Skye (Scotland) – London – Oxford – Duxford (near Cambridge)

2 1 Snowdonia; 2 Oxford; 3 Stratford-upon-Avon; 4 Brighton; 5 Duxford; 6 Nottingham; 7 Skye; 8 Edinburgh; 9 York; 10 Lake District

3 1 the Tyne; 2 Aberdeen; 3 Plymouth; 4 Birmingham; 5 Liverpool; 6 Mersey; 7 Isle of Man; 8 Lake District; 9 (the) Highlands; 10 Canterbury; 11 Cambridge; 12 Cardiff

Tapescript

Teacher's notes

Tomas: *We started out in London, of course, because London is near Heathrow airport and it's the capital city and a must for any visitor. After a few days in London we went to Brighton, on the south coast. That was really nice. The nightlife there was great and we loved being by the sea. We stayed there three days and then went on to Stratford-Upon-Avon. Emilia has to study English Literature at school and she wanted to see the birthplace of the famous William Shakespeare. I wasn't very interested but it was OK, and we only stayed one night. From Stratford we took a coach to Bath in the west of England. That was very beautiful too, but very crowded, and it was difficult to find accommodation. Next on our programme was Snowdonia in North Wales, which is a beautiful national park and a great area if you like walking, climbing, canoeing or pony trekking. We were lazy and took the Llanberis Mountain Railway up Mount Snowdon!*

We left Wales after two days and went back to London. There we went on The London Eye and had a fantastic view of the city in the early evening. In London we decided to visit the north of England and afterwards go on to Scotland. But let Emilia tell you the rest of the story.

Emilia: *Thanks, Tomas. OK, well, we arrived in York by train from Kings Cross. Tomas is mad about trains so he wanted to see the National Railway Museum. It was OK but after 2 hours I'd seen enough old steam locomotives to last me a lifetime. We also went to the Jorvik Viking Centre which we both really enjoyed. It's a museum I suppose, but it's like a journey back in time — you experience the sights, sounds and smells of an 8th century village.*

From York we crossed the border into Scotland. Our first destination was the capital, Edinburgh. There's a castle high up on the rocks with a spectacular view of the city.

We walked along Princes Street and The Royal Mile and I bought a tartan kilt in one of the shops!

Tomas wanted to go to Loch Ness after that because it's very famous but I thought it would be full of tourists. I thought it would be more interesting to visit one of the islands, and I persuaded Tomas to come to the Isle of Skye on the west coast. There's a romantic story about the Scottish prince, Bonnie Prince Charlie, who escaped to Skye after his army was beaten by the English in 1746. He crossed to the island in a small boat disguised as a woman. You know the song 'My Bonnie Lies Over the Ocean?' Well, that's about him. Anyway, after that we left Scotland. I wanted to go to the Lake District in the north-west of England which is a really beautiful area of lakes and mountains and small villages. The famous English poets Wordsworth and Coleridge lived there. Tomas wasn't keen: he wanted to go to Nottingham, in the North Midlands, because he

wanted to see Sherwood forest where Robin Hood lived (or so says the legend). We couldn't agree and in the end we didn't go to either — we went straight back to London. We had a couple more days left, so one day we went on a coach trip to Oxford, saw some of the old university colleges and did a bit of shopping. The next day Tomas persuaded me to go to Duxford near Cambridge. He was keen to see the Aviation Museum which has loads of old aeroplanes especially British and American fighter aircraft, and you can see some of them fly. I would have preferred to go sightseeing in London again, because there is so much to see there. In fact we could have spent the whole holiday there. I'm glad we didn't, though — we got a much wider picture of what Britain is like. We went to one island but saw three different countries!

Cultural References

a tartan kilt: a item of traditional Scottish dress. A kilt resembles a skirt, but it is worn by men as well as women. Tartan refers to the checked pattern of the material.
Llanberis: the spelling indicates this is a Welsh-language place name.
Robin Hood: a legendary outlaw who lived in Sherwood Forest near Nottingham in the 12th century and became famous for opposing tyranny and defending the poor.

Tube: Travel tips
Pre-Intermediate
1-3

■ Introduce the topic of travelling round cities. Ask students which cities they have visited and how they travelled around. Ask students about metros and undergrounds, crowded trains and platforms, which ones they have used and what the experience was like. Ask students about the best way to behave on the underground and what advice they would give to someone who hadn't used the tube before. Elicit vocabulary they are going to meet.
■ Hand out worksheets and ask students quickly to read the 9 tips and check for understanding.
■ Students do exercises 1, 2 and 3, individually or in pairs. Allow 20-25 minutes.
■ Check answers.

Answers
1 1 luggage, luggage; 2 backpack; 3 rush hours; 4 escalators; 5 platforms; 6 passengers, passengers; 7 yellow line; 8 air conditioning; 9 underground
2 a 1; b 3; c 4; d 7; e 6; f 5; g 9; h 2
3 a board; b in a hurry; c carry; d pull in and out; e all on its own; f carriage; g get past; h avoid; i porters

Teacher's notes

Cultural References

■ *Tips:* This word has several different meanings in English. Here it means pieces of advice

■ *The tube:* The London Underground is the oldest underground railway in the world. It was started in the 1840s and is still being extended today. It has a large network of different lines, covering a huge area of London and its suburbs.

Tube: Getting around   Intermediate

1

■ Introduce the topic by telling the students there are many places in central London with unusual names and it's important to recognize these names.

■ Play recording without the worksheet for students to hear names. Ask students to guess how these words are spelt.

■ Hand out the worksheet and the map for students to compare spellings.

■ Play recording again. Students repeat with correct pronunciation.

■ Play recording again without worksheets. Students write down spellings to see if they can remember them.

2

■ Ask students what they know about London, the famous places they have heard of or visited, what there is to see and what they think these places are like.

■ Allow 10 minutes for students to do this exercise.

■ Check answers.

3

■ Ask students to look at the tube map and explain about different lines and the need to change. Illustrate by explaining how to get to Mme Tussaud's.

■ Allow 15 minutes for students to do exercise 3 individually or in pairs.

■ Check answers.

4 & 5

■ Explain the task. Refer students to the places again, the times in brackets which are needed in each place, and the tube map.

■ Students work in pairs to plan the day. Allow 20 minutes.

■ Pairs discuss in groups of four before whole class discussion. Allow 10-15 minutes.

■ Class vote on the best plan.

Answers

2 1 Trafalgar Square; 2 Buckingham Palace; 3 Shakespeare's Globe Theatre; 4 Madame Tussaud's; 5 British Museum; 6 Harrod's Store; 7 Tower of London; 8 St. Paul's Cathedral; 9 Oxford Street; 10 Houses of Parliament

3

Place	Tube line	Change at:
Madame Tussaud's	Victoria & Jubilee	Green Park
Oxford Street	Victoria	–
British Museum	Victoria & Piccadilly	Green Park
Trafalgar Square	Circle/District & Northern	Embankment
Houses of Parliament	Circle/District	-
St Paul's Cathedral	Victoria and Central	Oxford Circus
Shakespeare's Globe	Circle/District & Northern	Embankment
The Tower of London	Circle/District	–
Buckingham Palace	Victoria	–
Harrod's Store	Circle/District & Piccadilly	South Kensington

Tapescript

a The Bakerloo Line, The Central Line, The Circle Line, The District Line, The Jubilee Line, The Metropolitan Line, The Northern Line, The Piccadilly Line, The Victoria Line.

b Baker Street, Charing Cross, Covent Garden, Gloucester Road, Holborn, Hyde Park Corner, Knightsbridge, Leicester Square, Marble Arch, Oxford Circus, Piccadilly Circus, Sloane Square, South Kensington, St. James's Park, Tottenham Court Road, Victoria, Waterloo, Westminster.

School Noticeboard: Notices
                                            Intermediate

1

■ Discuss what notices can be seen on a school or college notice board. What are they for? For example: to announce the date and place of a meeting, to advertise something for sale, to remind students about school rules, to notify students about an item lost or found.

■ Before starting the first activity, students skim-read all the notices, without stopping to look up unknown words.

■ Allow 10 minutes for the scanning activity.

■ Check answers with the class.

2

■ Students have to read the texts more carefully for this activity.

3

■ Give students another 5 minutes for the scanning and matching task.

■ Students can compare answers in pairs before class feedback.

4

■ This is another, more detailed reading activity. Allow 10 minutes for students to complete the task.

■ Extension. Using these notices as models, students could write their own notice in English for their classroom board. Possible topics include: Lost property, For Sale ads., Meetings, Shows & concerts.

Answers

1 2 Mrs Pritchard; 3 G Tunnicliffe; 4 Sam Morgan-Wendell; 5 Peter Tuck; 6 Marcus; 7 Jan Swirsky; 8

Teacher's notes

Mrs Capstick; 9 Mr Davies; 10 Jez Marshall; 11 the school counsellor

2 2 bat; 3 collage; 4 bullying; 5 kitten; 6 voluntary work; 7 published; 8 swap; 9 gig; 10 training; 11 costumes; 12 canteen; 13 Zip-Crackers

3 b 4; c 6; d 3; e 13; f 10; g 2; h 8; i 1; j 12

4 2 In the Music Annexe; 3 Grease; 4 Room 82B; 5 16; 6 Nothing; 7 English coursework folder; 8 4B; 9 7; 10 stationery and books; 11 Saturday mornings and Tuesday evenings; 12 They are fireworks

Language Notes and Cultural References

■ *housebound:* not able to leave the house because of illness or infirmity

■ *the red card:* put a stop to bullying (a reference to the red card in football, meaning a player must leave the field).

■ *Sam Morgan-Wendell:* It has become more common in Britain these days for children to take the surnames of both parents as many mothers keep their own surnames.

■ *Jez:* Jeremy. It's quite common for forenames to be abbreviated in this way.

■ *funtabulastic:* a invented word made by putting together 'fun' 'fabulous' and 'fantastic'.

■ *knockout:* really great

■ *Zip Crackers:* an imaginary firework

The School System: A typical school day
Pre-Intermediate

1

■ As an introduction to the topic, read the following statements aloud and ask students to say if they are True or False about secondary schools in Britain.
Lessons begin at 8 a.m. (False)
Students go to school on Saturday mornings. (False)
Students don't have homework until they are 15 years old. (False)
Most students have lunch at school. (True)
There are lessons in the afternoon. (True)

■ Students draw a simple picture of themselves (head and shoulders). This is not, of course, meant to test their drawing skills but simply a fun way into the main activity and a way of personalising it. (It shouldn't take more than a couple of minutes!)

■ Students answer Laura's questions in full sentences in order to practise the form of statements in the Present Simple (and Present Perfect) Tense.

■ Check answers and discuss the differences between their school day and Laura's.

■ Extension. Read aloud the following short text about school holidays in Britain.
Our school year consists of three terms: the Autumn Term, the Spring Term and the Summer Term. We get 2 weeks holiday at Easter, 6 weeks in the summer, 2 weeks at Christmas and we also get three half-term holidays of a week each.
Ask students: *How much holiday do British school students get a year?* Then get students to write a similar short text about their holidays and how their school year is divided.

Answers
Students' own answers.

Language Notes and Cultural References
Year 6 is the final year of Primary Education so pupils start secondary school in Year 7 at the age of 11. Laura is in Year 10 so she is 14 or 15 years old.

The form is the grouping of pupils for registration, which is done by the form tutor. This grouping usually lasts for one year, hence the expressions 1st Form (Year 7), 5th Form (Year 11), and so on.

Though Laura's day can be regarded as typical of British state secondary schools, there are of course many variations, both regionally and from school to individual school, e.g. in start and finish times and the length of lessons.

The School System: All about school
Intermediate

1

■ Use a map of Britain to show students where Brighton is.

■ Test or pre-teach the names in English of the main school subjects: Modern Languages (French, German, Spanish, etc.); Mathematics (Maths); English Language; English Literature; Science (Chemistry, Physics, Biology); Art & Design Technology; History; Geography; Religious Studies; Personal & Social Education ('Citizenship').

■ Students read Luke's letter and compare their own school experience and Luke's.

■ This exercise practises the structure of (wh-) questions in the Present Simple tense.

2

■ Guided writing. Using Luke's questions and his text as a model, students write about their school, the subjects they study and a bit about their hobbies and interests.

■ Remind students to check their work for grammar, spelling and punctuation errors before writing a final version.

Answers
1 2   Where do you live?
  3   Where is that/Brighton?
  4   Which school do you go to?
  5   Which year are you in?
  6   How old are your classmates?
  7   What does G.C.S.E. stand for?
  8   When do you take it/G.C.S.E.?
  9   How many subjects are you going to take?
  10 What subjects are you good at?
  11 What subjects don't you like?
  12 What's your favourite subject?

Teacher's notes

13 Which instrument do you play?

14 What's your band called/What's the name of your band?

15 How often do you/does the band rehearse?

16 Why are you practising hard (at the moment)?

The School System: Timetables
Pre-Intermediate/Intermediate

Though not essential, it is a recommended that the previous activity *All about school* is done before this one, as it provides important background information.

1

■ If not already done, pre-teach or revise the names of school subjects.

■ Look at Luke's incomplete timetable. Ask students to try to anticipate (but not write) what lessons might be in the blank spaces. For example, how many lesson of Science do you think he has? What about Religious Studies (R.S.)?

■ Play audio recording. Students listen and write.

■ Discuss any problems, but don't give solution yet.

■ Play recording again. Students compare their work in pairs.

■ Check answers.

2

■ Guided writing/structure practice. Students use the model sentences to compare their timetable with Luke's.

3

■ Discussion in pairs or groups. If your students need a more structured task, ask them to prepare a statement beginning: I prefer my school timetable because... or I prefer Luke's school timetable because... Each person in a group must think of a different reason from the others.

Answers

1	Monday	Tuesday	Wednesday	Thursday	Friday
1	History A11	RS A5	German L2	Science S15 Mrs Oakham	English A7
2	German L2	Science P8 Mr O'Connor	History A11	RS A5	History A11
3	English A7	Graphics D4	Maths S6 Mr Lane	Graphics D4	PSE A3
4	PE	Maths S6 Mr Lane	Science P8 Mr O'Connor	English A1	Maths P3 Miss Slade
5	PE	Science S15 Mrs Oakham	English A1	Maths P3 Miss Slade	Science B2 Mrs Marshall

Tapescript

I have English 4 times a week: period 3 on Monday in room A7, period 5 on Wednesday in A1, period 4 on Thursday, also in A1, and period 1 on Friday, back in A7.

I have German twice a week: that's on Monday period 2, and then on Wednesday period 1, both times in room L2.

I have Science five times a week (it's a core subject, and also I'm doing Double Science for G.C.S.E.). I don't have it on Monday at all, but I have it twice on Tuesday: period 2 in Room P8, with Mr O'Connor, and period 5 in S15 with Mrs Oakham. I'd better spell their names for you: O' Connor is spelt CAPITAL O-APOSTROPHE-CAPITAL C-O-N-N-O-R. And Oakham is spelt O-A-K-H-A-M. I have Science again on Wednesday, period 4, in Room P8 with Mr O'Connor, and on Thursday period 1 in room S15 with Mrs Oakham. Science is also my last lesson of the week, Friday period 5, this time in B2. It's with Mrs Marshall — that's M-A-R-S-H-A-L-L. She teaches us Human Biology.

My week starts with History — that's Monday morning, period 1. And I have another two periods of History: Wednesday, period 2 and Friday period 2. All of them are in room A11.

Maths is another core subject. I have four lessons a week with two different teachers. The first lesson is on Tuesday, period 4, and the second is on Wednesday, period 3. Both of these are with Mr Lane, spelt L-A-N-E, in room S6. Then I have 2 periods of Maths with Miss Slade in P3 — one on Thursday, period 5, and one on Friday period 4. Oh, her name is spelt S-L-A-D-E.

What else? Oh yes, I have P.E. (that means Physical Education) every Monday afternoon, periods 4 & 5. During the year we get to do a choice of activities, including gymnastics, athletics and basketball, plus of course football and cricket.

Oh, and there's Graphics. I nearly forgot! I have Graphics twice a week in room D4 — the first time on Tuesday, period 3, and the second time on Thursday, period 3.

I have two periods a week of R.S., which means Religious Studies. That's in room A5, and...oh, I haven't told you when it is. Let's see...R.S. is on Tuesday morning, period 1, and on Thursday morning, period 2.

On Friday, period 3, I have something called P.S.E., which means Personal and Social Education. It's about moral questions, erm, like how do we know the difference between right and wrong, and how to be a good citizen. Things like that. P.S.E. is in room A3.

OK? Well, that's my week at William Cobbett. As you see they keep us pretty busy! What about you? What's your week like?

Teacher's notes

The School System: Bullying
Upper Intermediate

Teachers will be aware that bullying is a sensitive issue which can provoke strong reactions in pupils, which may not be evident in the lesson. It may be necessary to guide the discussion part of this activity away from particular incidents and personalities in the pupils' own school, and focus on the general principles outlined in the text.

Note that the text, which is based on a real model in a secondary school handbook, is addressed both to parents and pupils.

1
- Set a five minute time limit for students to do this skimming activity. Remind them to look for the keywords: *physical, verbal, non-verbal, vulnerable.*

2-4
- These are more detailed vocabulary tasks. Students work individually and can then check their answers in pairs.

5
- This activity involves discussion in groups. If preferred, this can be left as the last activity.

6
- This gap-fill activity is a conclusion to the text, which can be done in the lesson or set as homework.

Answers
1 1 any two of these: hitting, prodding, pushing
  2 any two of these: nicknames, racist or sexist taunts, personal comments
  3 any one of these: taking sweets or money, damaging equipment
  4 students who are new, or different
2 2 withdrawn
  3 equipment
  4 bruising
3 1 inform
  2 victims
  3 blur
4 1 to get away with it
  2 bullies
  3 damage
6 awareness, investigating, listening, them, carefully, offer, bully, ensure, where

The School System: School uniform
Intermediate

1
- Before beginning the activity, students talk about the dress code in their school or other schools they know about. In most secondary schools in Britain uniform of some description is still a requirement. Ask students to guess: what the basic uniform might be for boys and girls, what items might be prohibited, which rules might cause most problems between pupil and school.
- Read the text. Answer questions about specific vocabulary items, e.g. *sling backs, platform heels, flesh-coloured, emblem, rugby shirt.*
- Writing. Students write about their own dress code, using Leah's questions and the vocabulary in the text 'School uniforms' as a guide. This can also be set as a homework.
- This writing exercise should follow the more friendly, informal style of Leah's e-mail, but will also involve use of some of the key language, e.g. *are not allowed.*
- Most students will enjoy talking about clothes, dress codes, the fairness or unfairness of prohibitions on this or that item.

2
- Allow 15 minutes for students to do the True/False exercise.
- Check answers.

Answers
2 2 False. The sweatshirts are only available from the school.
  3 True.
  4 False. They are black with a green band.
  5 True.
  6 False. One neck chain, one pair of stud earrings and two finger rings are permitted.
  7 False. Trainers are not permitted.
  8 True.
  9 True.
  10 True.
  11 False. His/her tutor will note this in the pupil's homework diary.
  12 False. Shoes with high heels are not permitted.
  13 True.

Store guide

1 Look at the store guide.

STORE GUIDE

GROUND FLOOR

◉ **MUSIC**
- CHART COMPILATIONS
- ROCK + POP
- R'N'B/HIP-HOP/SOUL
- METAL/HARDCORE/NU METAL
- DANCE
- JAZZ
- BLUES
- EASY LISTENING
- FOLK
- COUNTRY
- REGGAE
- WORLD
- CLASSICAL

◉ **CUSTOMER SERVICES**
- GIFT VOUCHERS
- EXCHANGES
- REFUNDS

FIRST FLOOR

◉ **VIDEO**
- CHART
- FEATURE FILMS
- DVD
- BUDGET
- MUSIC
- COMEDY
- CHILDREN'S
- SPECIAL INTEREST

◉ **GAMES**
- CHART
- PC
- CONSOLE

◉ **BOOKS**
◉ **POSTERS**
◉ **CLOTHING**
◉ **MOBILE PHONES**

2 Complete the conversations with phrases from the store guide.
There is an example to help you.

1 Joe: Have you got any CD collections of hit songs by different artists?
Assistant: You mean ..chart compilations.. ?
Joe: Yes, that's it.

2 Serena: I don't know what to buy for Jackie – I don't know what music she likes.
Mel: Why don't you buy her a ....; then she can come and choose something for herself?

3 Ahmed: I bought this DVD here and there's something wrong with it. The picture's not clear.
Assistant: I'm afraid we haven't got another copy of that film in stock. Would you like to .... it for another film?
Ahmed: No, I don't want another film. Could I have a ...., please?

4 Hiromi: Excuse me, do you sell T-shirts?
Assistant: Yes. You have to go to .... on the first floor.

5 Paulo: I'd like to buy a large picture for my bedroom wall.
Anna: You mean a .... ?
Paulo: Yes, that's right.

6 Alice: These videos are expensive, aren't they?
Kurt: There are some cheaper ones over there in the section marked ....

Music vocabulary

---

1 Jeff is taking part in a pub quiz. It's all about styles of music. Read the questions, then look at Jeff's answers. Are they right or wrong? Can you do better than Jeff?

Questionmaster:

1 This word means a kind of traditional music which originally came from the common people. It's usually played on acoustic instruments, like the guitar, mandolin or fiddle (violin).

....

2 This word means the music that accompanies a film. There are many famous examples. People see a film and love the music, so they want to buy this on a CD or a tape. ....

3 This is a type of music that came from the West Indies, particularly the island of Jamaica. It's got a distinctive rhythm that people love. Bob Marley was a famous singer of this style of music. ....

4 This music is very fast and very loud. Often the singer sounds as if he is screaming the words. The bands who play it often wear black and have long hair. ....

5 This is a very wide category because it includes music from many different countries, not just Britain or America. It reflects the people and the culture of that country. ....

Music Quiz: Jeff

1 Jazz
2 Soundtrack
3 r'n'b
4 Dance Hip hop
5 World music

---

2 Unjumble the words to find what these people bought. Then match the word with the picture.

1 "I've bought this Buffy the Vampire Slayer video. It's a 3-tape ....._boxset_........." **S T O B E X** (e)

2 "I got *It's my turn to play*! It's a .... for 4-6 players." **D R O B A   M E G A** ( )

3 "Look, I bought this CD of Gorillaz. They're great, but some of the .... are very strong. There's a special sticker on it, to warn parents." **C R I L Y S** ( )

4 "I bought some .... CDs to record music on. This pack of 5 cost £3.99." **L N K A B** ( )

5 "I got these .... for my personal stereo. They're very light and you can fold them and put them in your pocket." **S H E P E D H O A N** ( )

6 "I'm really pleased - I managed to get this game for my .... It's called "Star Warriors: Adventures in Time and Space". **T P A S Y N O I L A T** ( )

a b c d e f

Videos

---

1 Annie is talking to Denise, a girl she met on holiday. Divide the text into Annie's words and Denise's words. Add punctuation (full stops, capital letters, commas).

I want to buy a video for my younger sister what about stuart little 2 that's very good no she's not that young well what about true lies with arnold schwarzenegger no way she hates action movies then perhaps she'd like this harry potter video no i don't think so she's not into all that stuff about witches and wizards and magic spells your sister sounds difficult to please yes she is does she like romantic films yes she does actually well how about this one shakespeare in love it's about how the young poet got inspired to write romeo and juliet it sounds good she has to study shakespeare at school so this will be just right for her

Annie: I want to buy a video for my younger sister.

Denise: What about 'Stuart Little 2'? That's very good.

Annie:

Denise:

Annie:

Denise:

Annie:

Denise:

Annie:

Denise:

Annie:

Denise:

Annie:

---

2 Practise the conversation with a partner.

Supermarket layout

1 Bob's shopping list is not very well organised. Look at the plan of the supermarket and write Bob's list out again in a better order, to save him time. You can work in pairs.

Bob's list

olive oil
2 litres of semi-skimmed milk
2 salmon steaks
multipack of Pepsi
honey-coated cornflakes
plum tomatoes
cooked ham from the deli
decaffeinated coffee
microwave meal (chicken curry?)
half dozen large eggs (free range)
multipack of crisps (assorted flavours)
sparkling mineral water
1 kg carrots
nectarines (2 punnets for the price of one!)
1/2 kg minced beef
Top of the Pops magazine
4 tins of baked beans
tutti frutti ice cream
large wholemeal loaf
carton of fresh orange juice

Your list

1 ....
2 ....
3 ....
4 ....
5 ....
6 ....
7 ....
8 ....
9 ....
10 ....
11 ....
12 ....
13 ....
14 ....
15 ....
16 ....
17 ....
18 ....
19 ....
20 ....

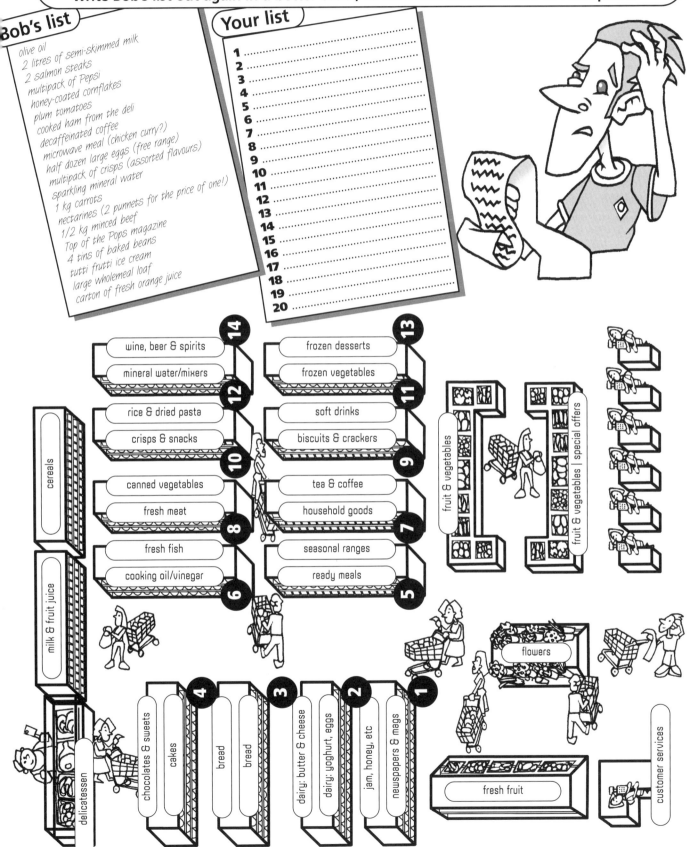

Supermarket layout

2 Look at the plan of the supermarket again. Complete the dialogues. Sometimes you have to write the question, and sometimes you have to write the answer. The first two have been done for you.

1 A Excuse me. Where can I find the cereals, please?
   B *On the back wall, just to the right of the milk.*

2 A *Excuse me. Where can I find cakes?*
   B In aisle 4, on the left, opposite bread.

3 A Could you tell me where the cheese crackers are, please?
   B ....

4 A ....
   B It's in aisle 8, opposite fresh fish.

5 A Do you know where the mineral water is, please?
   B ....

6 A ....
   B It's with the milk, on the back wall, between the deli and cereals.

7 A Excuse me. Where can I find honey?
   B ....

8 A ....
   B It's with cooking oils, in aisle 6, opposite cakes and bread.

9 A Excuse me. Do you sell fresh flowers?
   B ....

10 A ....
    B It's just on the left as you go into the store.

3 Read the dialogues with a partner for practice.

4 With your partner, make up some more questions and answers about things in the supermarket.

Q ....
A ....
Q ....
A ....
Q ....
A ....
Q ....
A ....

5 Work in a small group.

You are supermarket managers. You have to think of a promotion/special offer that will attract more customers to your store. Remember, your aim is to make a profit, so it shouldn't be too expensive! Present your promotion to the whole class.

At the end, the whole class should vote for the most interesting, original and attractive promotion, which will also make the store successful!

Vocabulary

1 🎧 Nathalie is staying in Britain at the moment because she wants to improve her English. She has just come back from the supermarket and is talking to her English friend, David. Listen to the recording and look at the pictures. Write the missing word on the items Nathalie talks about.

2 🎧 Listen. Are the sentences 1 - 12 true or false? If the sentence is false, try to correct it.

1 Nathalie has learnt some new English vocabulary from her trip to the supermarket. ✓ **true** ⬤ **false**
....

2 A tub is a container for toothpaste. ⬤ **true** ✓ **false**
A tub is a container for butter or margarine.
....

3 Salad dressing contains oil and vinegar. ⬤ **true** ⬤ **false**
....

4 David doesn't like fudge. ⬤ **true** ⬤ **false**
....

5 Nathalie has bought some fudge. ⬤ **true** ⬤ **false**
....

6 David recommends that Nathalie try cheddar cheese. ⬤ **true** ⬤ **false**
....

7 You must add water to squash before you drink it. ⬤ **true** ⬤ **false**
....

8 David thinks squash is a horrible drink. ⬤ **true** ⬤ **false**
....

9 Cutlery means cups, plates and bowls. ⬤ **true** ⬤ **false**
....

10 A cheese grater is an example of software. ⬤ **true** ⬤ **false**
....

11 Ginger beer is non-alcoholic. ⬤ **true** ⬤ **false**
....

12 Nathalie didn't know the meaning of the word *ginger* until she tried ginger beer. ⬤ **true** ⬤ **false**
....

Labels and instructions

1 Match the directions to the product by drawing a line.

2 Which products do these people need? Write the correct letter in the spaces.

1 Harry's lamp doesn't work. ....j.........
2 Sarah has a terrible headache. ....
3 Giorgio wants to make a phone call. ....
4 Anna feels like eating something sweet. .... or ....
5 Dona has cut her finger. ....
6 Bela wants a new pair of casual trousers. ....
7 Paulo's hair is dirty. ....
8 Marek wants a cold drink. .... or ....

Sending things abroad

> **1** Read this information about sending things to other countries from a British post office. Then look at the wordsearch. Find the words to complete the definitions below.

SENDING POST ABROAD: HAVE YOU GOT THE RIGHT POSTAGE?

Letters
You can send virtually anything that you would normally send through the domestic post, including postcards. The maximum weight you can send is 2kg.

Small Packets
Use this service to send goods, gifts and trade samples, audio/video tapes, magnetic tapes, and photographs. You can include a letter, invoice or other document if it relates to the contents of the item.

Printed Papers
Use this service to send advertisements, books, calendars, catalogues, diaries, directories, greetings cards, illustrations, magazines, maps, musical scores, newspapers, order/subscription forms, leaflets and pamphlets, plans, postcards, posters, price lists, printed drawings and notices, proofs, prospectuses and timetables.

```
T  H  G  I  F  T
E  P  R  S  O  C
G  T  E  O  P  A
O  F  E  W  S  L
D  C  T  E  T  E
S  A  I  I  A  N
M  A  N  G  G  D
P  O  G  H  E  A
N  I  S  N  A  R
D  B  C  R  Y  R
A  J  A  O  A  E
D     R  A     D
        D  C     D
```

1 A present you give someone. ....gift.................

2 How heavy something is. ....

3 A list of all the days, weeks, months in a year. ....

4 A book with all the days of the year. ....

5 Something you send people at Christmas or on special occasions (2 words). ....

6 A big picture you put on your wall. ....

7 Anywhere in the world that is not your country. ....

8 The cost of sending something by post. ....

9 Products, things you can buy. ....

Sending things abroad

2 Now read this information about sending things by airmail and complete the table below.

Zones

If you're sending an item abroad by airmail, you'll need to know the right postage and that depends on your destination country's zone.

The Royal Mail divides the world into three zones:

Zone	Coverage
Europe	All countries in Europe including the Republic of Ireland
Rest of World Zone 1	South America, North America, Canada, the Middle East, Africa, parts of Asia including the Indian sub-continent, most of southeast Asia and Hong Kong
Rest of World Zone 2	The rest of the world outside Zone 1 and Europe comprising countries and territories in Asia and Australasia.

Airmail Prices

Weight under	LETTERS Europe Zone	Zone 1	Zone 2	SMALL PACKETS Europe Zone	Zone 1	Zone 2	PRINTED PAPER Europe Zone	Zone 1	Zone 2
postcards	£0.37	£0.42	£0.42						
10g	£0.37	£0.47	£0.47						
20g	£0.37	£0.68	£0.68						
40g	£0.52	£1.05	£1.12						
60g	£0.68	£1.42	£1.56						
80g	£0.84	£1.79	£2.00						
100g	£0.99	£2.16	£2.44	£0.90	£1.20	£1.21	£0.78	£1.20	£1.21
120g	£1.14	£2.52	£2.88	£1.00	£1.37	£1.41	£0.86	£1.37	£1.41
140g	£1.29	£2.88	£3.32	£1.10	£1.54	£1.61	£0.94	£1.54	£1.61
160g	£1.44	£3.24	£3.76	£1.20	£1.71	£1.81	£1.02	£1.71	£1.81
180g	£1.59	£3.60	£4.20	£1.29	£1.89	£2.01	£1.10	£1.89	£2.01
200g	£1.74	£3.96	£4.64	£1.38	£2.07	£2.21	£1.18	£2.07	£2.21
300g	£2.49	£5.77	£6.84	£1.83	£2.97	£2.97	£1.63	£2.97	£2.97
400g	£3.24	£7.62	£9.04	£2.28	£3.87	£3.87	£2.03	£3.87	£3.87

	Item	Type	Zone	Total Cost
1	Two postcards to Madrid	letter	Europe	£0.74
2	A present of English tea to Milan (300g)			
3	A set of photos to Sydney, Australia (180g)			
4	Two posters of David Beckham to Argentina (120g, 160g)			
5	Five postcards to New York			
6	A birthday card to Berlin (140g)			
7	A video tape to Cairo (200g)			
8	A present of a diary to Toronto (180g)			
9	Two English magazines to Delhi (200g each)			
10	Six Christmas cards to New Zealand (2 of 80g, 2 of 100g, 2 of 120g)			

A conversation

1 🎧 **Laura has some things she wants to take to the post office. Read the dialogue. Then listen to her conversation with the cashier. Underline and correct everything you hear which is different.**

3

Cashier number ~~thirteen~~, please.

Crash number seven, please.

Cashier:	Good afternoon.
Laura:	Hello. I want to send these postcards to Italy, please.
Cashier:	How much have you got?
Laura:	Let me see, three, four, and this one, five, please.
Cashier:	Five at twenty-seven each, that's … one pound thirty-five.
Laura:	OK, and I've got this packet of tissues.
Cashier:	Is this for Italy too?
Laura:	Yes, that's right.
Cashier:	Can you put it on the sales, please?
Laura:	There?
Cashier:	No, over here. That one's thirty-eight.
Laura:	One thirty-eight. And these Italian newspapers too …. on the escalator?
Cashier:	Please … they weigh 500 grams so that's another two pounds and thirty-three pence. So, altogether that comes to four pound six, please. Thanks, twenty pounds …. fourteen thirty-seven change. Just take the packet and papers through to me. Right.
Laura:	Thanks, bye.
Cashier:	Thank you.

2 **Check your answers with a friend. Now read the correct conversation together. When you have read one part of the dialogue, change roles.**

3 **Work with a friend. Imagine you are at a post office in England. One of you wants to send some things home, and the other one is the cashier. Have a conversation using the information for the correct prices. You can use these ideas or your own:**

- *two posters*
- *a video tape*
- *a sweater*
- *a packet of photographs*
- *three postcards*
- *a magazine*
- *a birthday card*
- *a heavy (3 kg) parcel of books*

At the clothes shop

1 🎧 Hannah and Daniel are clothes shopping. Listen to their conversations. Which clothes do they choose? Tick (✔) the correct picture for each conversation.

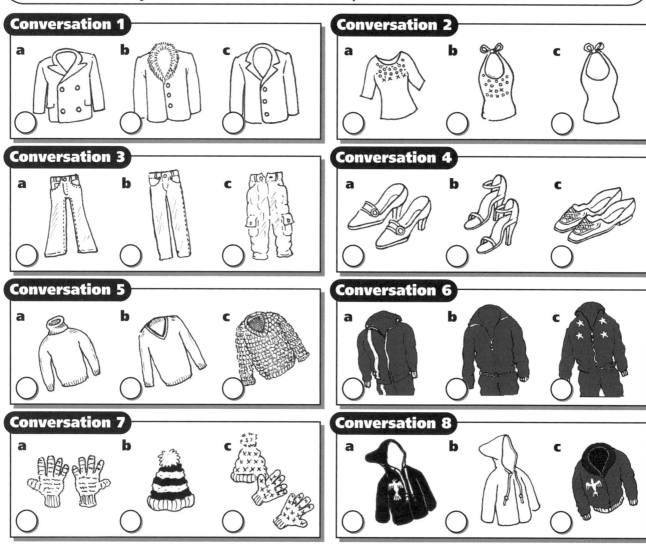

Conversation 1
a   b   c

Conversation 2
a   b   c

Conversation 3
a   b   c

Conversation 4
a   b   c

Conversation 5
a   b   c

Conversation 6
a   b   c

Conversation 7
a   b   c

Conversation 8
a   b   c

2 🎧 Listen to the recording again and complete these sentences using words from the dialogues.

1 He doesn't like the ......*fur*........ collar.

2 He'd prefer a single- .... jacket.

3 Halterneck tops don't .... her.

4 He likes the bead .... on the front.

5 These jeans are too .... ; he's after some baggy ones.

6 Not .... , just baggy. You know, ... -fitting.

7 She doesn't want shoes with high ....

8 The chunky-knit jumper makes her ....

9 She doesn't want a track suit with stars or stripes on it, she wants a completely .... one.

10 He's going to buy his mother a .... hat and gloves.

11 He'd rather have a .... top than a blouson jacket.

12 He likes the one with the eagle .... on the front.

At the clothes shop

3 Fill each gap with a word or phrase from the box.

1 I've put on so much weight my clothes don't (fit) me any more.

2 I never wear red, it just doesn't ( ) me.

3 You've got a new jacket, you just need a pair of trousers to ( ) ( ) it.

4 A: I'd like to ( ) ( ) this dress, please.

   B: Sure. There's a fitting room over there.

5 I like this top, but it's too small. Have you got it in a bigger ( ) ?

6 You can't go out ( ) like that, you'll catch a cold. Go and put a pullover on.

7 What are you ( ) to the party tonight?

8 A: Do you sell silk scarves?

   B: Yes. You want WOMEN'S ( ) on the 2nd floor.

9 INSTRUCTIONS: Take care of your swimsuit: ( ) thoroughly in cold water immediately after use.

10 Casual ( ) are OK for a party, but this is a wedding so you will have to dress ( )

11 A: I'd like to buy some new trainers.

   B: OK. I know a good ( ) shop in West Street.

> try on   wearing   rinse
> fit   smartly   accessories
> clothes   size   go with
> dressed   sportswear   suit

4 Underline the odd one out in each group. Explain why the word is different.

1 sandals   trainers   <u>slippers</u>   boots   ....They are only worn indoors.........

2 suede   leather   shiny   wool   ....

3 jeans   trousers   leggings   tights   ....

4 gloves   skirt   earrings   belt   ....

5 striped   frilly   checked   spotted   ....

6 x-large   reduced   medium   small   ....

The burger bar

1 Look at the picture of the burger bar. Use the words from the box to label the food.

mayonnaise   tomatoes
pineapple   chilli sauce   onions
cheese   garlic sauce   lettuce
mushrooms   ketchup   mustard

1 ....
2 ....
3 ....
4 ....
5 ....
6 ....
7 ....
8 ....
9 ....
10 ....
11 ....

2 Laura and her friends are at the burger bar. Read the menu and the information below and guess what each person orders.

1 Laura doesn't eat meat. *a veggieburger*

2 Jamie has only got £3. ....

3 Rachael doesn't like green salad.
....

4 Daniel is really hungry. ....

5 Kylie likes really hot food but doesn't
like cheese. ....

6 Kieron loves all kinds of fruit.
....

7 Abbie likes garlic but doesn't like
mushrooms. ....

8 Jordan hates onions. ....

Burgers

Original   **£2.95**
lettuce, onion, ketchup

Cheeseburger   **£3.20**
lettuce, onion, ketchup,
cheese

Hawaiian   **£3.05**
lettuce, onion, ketchup,
pineapple

Chilliburger   **£3.05**
lettuce, onion, chilli sauce

Mexican   **£3.30**
lettuce, chilli sauce,
cheese

Mustardburger   **£3.40**
lettuce, onion, mustard

All Star   **£3.50**
lettuce, onion, tomato,
mayonnaise, cheese

Garlicburger   **£3.05**
lettuce, onion, garlic sauce

Veggieburger   **£3.20**
non-meat slice, lettuce,
onion

Mushroom Supreme **£3.30**
onion, mushrooms, garlic
sauce

3 What would you have in your favourite burger? What filling, salad, vegetables or sauces
would you choose? When you have written your answer compare it with a friend.

My favourite burger:

....

....

The pizza restaurant

1 Look at this pizza menu. Match the pizza names with their ingredients.

Italian Crust Pizzas

1 Margherita £4.70
2 Hawaiian £5.80
3 Hot 'n' spicy £5.90
4 Seafood £6.15
5 Vegetarian £5.90
6 Meatlover £6.15
7 American Two-timer £5.80
8 Chicken 'n' mushroom £5.80
9 Garlic treat £5.80
10 Chef's special £6.45

a onion, pepperoni, spicy beef, chilli

b chicken, mushroom, green pepper

c cheese, tomato

d garlic, onion, olives

e chicken, ham, spicy beef, pepperoni, salami

f prawns, tuna, anchovies, olives

g mushroom, ham, pineapple

h mushroom, onion, green pepper, tomatoes

i mushroom, green pepper, onion, salami, pepperoni, ham, spicy beef, garlic

j double mushroom, double pepperoni

1 Margherita c   **2 Hawaiian** ○   **3 Hot 'n' spicy** ○   **4 Seafood** ○

5 Vegetarian ○   **6 Meatlover** ○   **7 American Two-timer** ○

8 Chicken 'n' mushroom ○   **9 Garlic treat** ○   **10 Chef's special** ○

2 Here are some more things you can order in the restaurant. Write the number of the correct picture next to the item on the menu.

Extras,
Desserts and Drinks

b Side salad	£1.50
○ Garlic mushrooms	£2.00
○ Garlic bread	£1.20
○ Fries	£1.00
○ Onion rings	£1.25
○ Chocolate fudge cake	£2.00
○ Ice cream (vanilla, chocolate, fudge, raspberry)	£1.70
○ Apple pie and ice cream	£2.00
○ Can of cola	£0.75
○ Milkshake (strawberry, chocolate, banana)	£1.50

The pizza restaurant

3 🎧 You are the waiter/waitress in the pizza restaurant. Laura and four of her friends come in and order a meal. Listen to what they say and write their order on your notepad.

Italian Crust Pizzas

pizzas

extras

drinks

desserts

4 At the end of the meal you bring the bill for Laura and her friends. How much have they spent together? How much have they each spent?

£ Total bill

£ Laura

£ Daniel

£ Rachael

£ Abbie

£ Jamie

Ratings

CINE WEST BRIGHTON MARINA
PROGRAMMES FOR WEEK COMMENCING FRIDAY 27TH SEPTEMBER

MY BIG FAT GREEK WEDDING (PG)
11.10   1.30   3.40   6.00   8.30
(Late show: Sat 10.45)

SIGNS (12A)
Contains moderate violence
11.00 (not Sat)   12.30   1.30   3.00   4.00   5.45   6.30   8.30
8.45 (Sun to Thurs)   9.10 (Fri & Sat)   11.10 (late show Sat only)

SPY KIDS 2: THE ISLAND OF LOST DREAMS (U)
11.10 (Sat & Sun only)

SWIMFAN (12A)
Contains moderate sex and violence
1.30   6.30 (no shows Weds)

INSOMNIA (15)
2.35   5.20   8.05   (Sun 5.20 & 8.05 only)

PRICES
Early Bird shows starting before 12 noon: all tickets £2.95
Adults: £4.75 for shows starting before 5.00pm,
£5.50 all other shows
Children: £3.60; **OAP:** £3.90

ADVANCE BOOKING & INFORMATION 0870 555 1212

---

1 In Britain every film has a certificate rating which tells the public who is allowed to see it. Look at the films above and complete this ratings chart with the correct symbol.

SYMBOL	DEFINITION
	No-one under the age of 15 is allowed to see this film.
(12)	No children under the age of 12 can see this film.
	Children under the age of 12 can only see this film if they are accompanied by an adult.
	This film may not be suitable for a child under the age of 12. It is for the parents to decide if they want their child to see this film, so it depends on parental guidance.
	Anyone can go to see this film, it has a universal certificate.

---

2 Now look at the advertisement again and write your answers to these questions.

1 Can you go to see 'Swimfan' every day of the week? ....

2 If you miss the 3.40 performance of 'My Big Fat Greek Wedding' how long will you have to wait till the next one? ....

3 What time is the first show of 'Insomnia' on Sunday? ....

4 What time is the last show of 'Signs' on Friday? ....

5 What is the cheapest price for two adults and two children to go to see 'Spy Kids 2'? ....

6 What is the cheapest price for two adults and two children to go to see 'My Big Fat Greek Wedding'? ....

7 What is the cheapest price for one adult and two children to go to see 'Swimfan'? ....

8 How much will two adults save by going to the 4.00 performance of 'Signs' instead of the 5.45 one? ....

Film reviews • 1

Title	Story	Our Verdict
Signs (12A) Mel Gibson, Joaquin Phoenix	In a closed Pennsylvanian community, farmer Graham Hess (Gibson) and his two young children and little brother experience strange things when a crop circle appears in their field. Is it a sign of aliens or something closer to home?	With a powerful [1] ...*performance*... from Gibson and tense direction from Shyamalan, *Signs* gets under your skin with shock after shock. The [2] .... is not always [3] .... , but stay with it and you will be on the edge of your seat! ★ ★ ★ ★ ★
Insomnia (15) Al Pacino, Robin Williams	Veteran policeman Will Dormer (Pacino) and his young partner travel to Alaska to find a murderer. But Dormer has a secret from the past which the murderer uses to make sure the hunter becomes the hunted.	This film is a real [4] .... The tension builds as Will comes under more and more pressure. Superb [5] .... by Pacino makes the [6] .... of Will completely believable. The plot twists and turns under Nolan's skilful [7] .... ★ ★ ★ ★
Spy Kids 2 (U) Alex Vega, Daryl Sabara	Child agents Carmen and Juni Cortez (Vega and Sabara) have to find a strange machine on an island created by mad scientist Romero. The island is full of crazy creatures and our heroes must find the machine before their enemies, Gary and Gertie Giggles.	This film is great [8] .... if you forget about the silly plot. It is as exciting as their first [9] .... with some fantastic [10] .... The comedy and the cheeky performances of the youngsters give you everything you want in a [11] .... ★ ★ ★ ★
My Big Fat Greek Wedding (PG) Nia Vardalos, John Corbett	Vardalos stars as unexciting Toula who attracts handsome teacher Ian Miller (Corbett). Toula doesn't want to tell her parents about Ian because he isn't Greek. But when Ian asks her to marry him the bomb drops! Ian has no idea of the chaos to follow!	With a heart of gold, this is a charming [12] .... The energetic [13] .... and the honest [14] .... make the film funny and very watchable. Vardalos is wonderful in the [15] .... while the rest of the actors are superb. ★ ★ ★
Swimfan (12A) Jesse Bradford, Erika Christensen	Ben Cronin (Bradford) is a high-school star with everything - brains, looks, a loving girlfriend, and a successful swimming record. But when new girl Madison, (Christensen) comes on the scene, things soon go out of control.	Another high-school [16] .... , *Swimfan* is too predictable to be very [17] .... The girls will enjoy looking at Bradford but the plot is weak and the [18] .... of the film is ridiculous. ★ ★

Film reviews • 1

1 Laura and Jamie want to go and see a film. They look at the film reviews in the newspaper. Read the film reviews and write the answers to the questions below.

1 Which film is a comedy adventure? ....

2 Which two films are romances? ....

3 Which two films are thrillers? ....

4 Which film takes place in the far North of the USA? ....

5 Which film is about the relationship between parents and children? ....

6 Which film has two sets of brothers and sisters? ....

7 Which film is about a possibly supernatural experience? ....

8 Which film is about teenagers? ....

9 Laura and Jamie are fourteen years old. They want to see something which is exciting but will also make them laugh. Which film would you recommend for them and why? ....
....

10 Which film would you like to see and why? ....
....

2 Now match these words from the box with their correct meanings:

cast
performance
lead role
family movie
~~thriller~~
direction
special effects
comedy
plot
character
entertaining
script
teen movie
fun
ending
believable
adventure
acting

1 a very exciting, frightening film
 thriller
 ....

2 the end of a film
 ....

3 the dialogue of a film
 ....

4 a film for teenagers
 ....

5 the story of a film
 ....

6 the actors in a film
 ....

7 a person in a film
 ....

8 the most important person in a film
 ....

9 what an actor does
 ....

10 a funny film
 ....

11 something you think is true
 ....

12 the way an actor acts in a film
 ....

13 when something makes you feel happy
 ....

14 technical aspects of a film
 ....

15 what a director does
 ....

16 a film for everybody in a family
 ....

17 when a film keeps you interested all the time
 ....

18 an exciting story that may include travel
 ....

3 Complete the reviews by writing the correct word in each gap.

Film reviews • 2

The Top Five Teen Movies on Video!

At Number 1, it's ... **Legally Blonde**

Who's in it?
Reese Witherspoon, Luke Wilson and Selma Blair

What happens?
When Elle (Witherspoon), whose main interests in life seem to be shopping and clothes, gets the push from her boyfriend, she goes to law school to try and win him back.

What makes it so great?
Dumb blonde is not so dumb - in fact, not only has she got brains, she gets her man and gives him what he deserves!!

Number 2 is **Clueless**

Who's in it?
Alicia Silverstone and Paul Rudd

What happens?
Cher (Silverstone) goes shopping, gives her best friend a makeover, goes shopping, arranges the lives of her teachers, goes shopping, falls in love, goes shopping and says 'Like, whatever' a lot.

What makes it so great?
Great characters, sharp script, big laughs and an air of feel-good fun. It is Jane Austen's 'Emma', brought right up-to-date.

Cruel Intentions comes in at number 3

Who's in it?
Sarah Michelle Gellar, Ryan Phillippe and Reese Witherspoon

What happens?
Dangerous stepsister Kathryn (Gellar) bets Sebastian (Phillippe) that he cannot seduce sweet, innocent Annette (Witherspoon). Who will win in the end?

What makes it so great?
Based on the classic 'Dangerous Liaisons', this is a very good-looking film, full of scandal, scheming and bad intentions.

Romeo and Juliet is number 4

Who's in it?
Leonardo DiCaprio and Claire Danes

What happens?
Shakespeare's story of star-crossed lovers with guns and gangsters. Verona Beach, Florida is the setting for this tragic love-story of two young people whose love is not to be.

What makes it so great?
Fast-paced action, top music, Shakespeare's words and pretty stars.

At number 5 it's **Crossroads**

Who's in it?
Britney Spears and Anton Mount

What happens?
Three girls and one mysterious guy take a road trip across the USA and get themselves into plenty of trouble on the way.

What makes it so great?
Britney and her songs.

---

1 Look at the reviews and find the following:

1 Two films with Reese Witherspoon ....

2 Three films based on classic stories ....

3 Two films to enjoy for the music ....

4 Two films to enjoy for the good conversation ....

5 The funniest film ....

6 The saddest film ....

---

2 Now write your own film review. Think of a film you have really enjoyed seeing. Write about it using these headings:

Film title: ....   What makes it so great? ....

Who's in it? ....

What happens? ....

....

---

3 Do you have your own top five favourite films? Write your list and compare it with your friends.

....

....

....

Programmes and listings

> **1** Here are the names of some different kinds of TV programmes. Read each definition and put the letters in the correct order to make the name of the programme.

1 A true programme about something in real life.   **nurdmotyaec**

(d)(o)(c)(u)(m)(e)(n)(t)(a)(r)(y)

2 A serial, continuing story shown more than once a week   **poas**
about the lives of families, friends, neighbours or workmates.

( )( )(a)( )

3 A situation comedy, usually a half-hour programme, with a different   **mitocs**
amusing story each week about a family or group of people.

(s)( )( )( )( )( )

4 Animated drawings, usually about animals or characters in   **rotcona**
fantasy situations.

( )( )(r)( )( )(n)( )

5 In this programme, a TV host interviews different famous guests.   **oklahtsw**

( )( )(k)(s)( )( )( )

6 A play or story, often about people who have problems in their lives.   **ramad**

( )( )( )(a)( )

7 These programmes tell us about what is happening in the world   **snwe**
at the moment

( )( )(w)( )

8 A programme about animals,   **fliedwil**
birds and fish.

( )( )( )(d)( )( )( )(e)

9 A programme which   **yemdoc**
makes you laugh.

( )( )(m)( )( )( )

10 In this show, people   **eoshgwam**
compete for prizes.

( )(a)( )( )( )( )( )( )

11 These programmes are about   **rposts**
activities like football, tennis or motor racing.

( )( )( )( )(t)( )( )

Programmes and listings

2 Look at these TV listings. Write the type of programme next to each one. Sometimes you can use more than one word. <u>Underline</u> the words which tell you what kind of programme it is.

1 Ch 4 6.00 **Friends The One Where Everyone Rushes Around:** A repeat of one your <u>funniest</u> favourite <u>episodes</u>. Monica and Rachel try to get their apartment back but nothing goes right with <u>hilarious</u> results!

comedy, sitcom

2 ITV1 3.00 **The Goal Rush:** Including the latest scores at every match in the Premiership. Angus Scott presents, with studio guests Ron Atkinson, John Barnes and Jim Beglin.

3 BBC1 9.00 **Merseybeat:** The Liverpool cops are back with Susan preparing for the enquiry into the death of Guy Morgan.

4 ITV1 7.30 **Play Your Cards Right:** Bruce Forsyth returns for more fun with more contestants. This week, four couples compete for the big prize.

5 ITV1 8.00 **Tonight With Trevor McDonald:** More exclusive interviews with the people behind the headlines.

6 BBC1 8.00 **Holby City:** Tom's patient returns to Holby needing urgent medical treatment, but the situation gets difficult when the police arrive wanting to talk to him. Will the doctors and nurses survive yet another crisis?

7 Ch 5 7.00 **Live With...Chris Moyles:** Tonight host Chris chats to actor Pierce Brosnan.

8 BBC2 9.00 **Great Britons:** Actor Alan Davies tells us why he thinks former Beatle, John Lennon, should take his place up there with Shakespeare, Winston Churchill and Princess Diana. This is the true story of the man who represented a new generation, communicating hope, peace and love in a language understood all over the world - music.

9 BBC1 9.00 **The Life Of Mammals: A Winning Design:** David Attenborough looks at why mammals are the most successful animals on the planet and investigates the strange wildlife of Australia.

10 ITV1 7.30 **Coronation Street:** After the events of last Friday, Audrey tries to tell daughter Gail about her problems. Sally meets a handsome stranger while Kevin takes a break from the family.

11 BBC1 8.05 **Looney Toons:** More crazy characters and their amazing adventures!

3 Look at the programmes again and <u>underline</u> the correct information in these sentences.

1 In Britain there are **3 / 4 / 5** normal (terrestrial) television **lines / channels / canals**.

2 Each story in a sitcom is called **an episode / a series / a plot**.

3 In a gameshow, different **fighters / contestants / gamers** **chat / represent / compete** for prizes.

4 A talkshow **host / guest / ghost** **makes / chats / says** with famous people.

5 There is often a life-or-death **survive / crisis / treatment** in **nurse / doctor / hospital** dramas.

Programmes and listings

4 Here are some titles of TV programmes. Write a short description for each one using the words given.

1 BBC1 10.20 **Parkinson**

....

....

....

....

....

host/Michael Parkinson/guests/Richard Gere/Halle Berry

2 BBC2 6.00 **The Simpsons**

....

....

....

....

....

cartoon/family/episode/adventure

3 ITV1 8.00 **The Bill**

....

....

....

....

....

police drama/episode/hunt/killer/Detective Inspector Nixon/crisis

4 Ch 4 7.00 **News & Weather**

....

....

....

....

....

one hour/full stories/interviews/today/headlines

5 BBC1 8.00 **My Family**

....

....

....

....

....

sitcom/episode/funny/Ben and Susan/family/crazy weekend

6 BBC2 8.00 **Europe Now**

....

....

....

....

....

documentary/investigates/Italy/people/Italian situation/future

5 Write down the names of your favourite TV programmes. Think about what you like and what you don't like on TV. Now work with a friend and talk about what you have written.

My favourite TV programmes: ....

....

Why I like them: ....

....

What I don't like on TV: ....

....

6 Now imagine you are going to stay in and watch TV for the evening.
Work with a friend and plan what you would like to see. Write the times, the names and a short description of the programmes you plan to see.

....

....

....

....

....

Reviews

1 Read about the computer games in the catalogue. Which game would you choose?

Can you steal the Crown Jewels?
You are the hero who has to break through the tough defences of the Tower of London and steal the Crown Jewels before the bad guy does. And you're going to leave a set of bugged replica Jewels there to trap him. Start by tracking your way through the Tower's sewers – recreated with horrible accuracy!

Traitors' Gate £29.99

Battle of the robots
Watch the sparks fly as your own robots battle together in the arena! You design the robots yourself choosing from several different designs and with plenty of amazing equipment. The excitement never stops, as you face up to different opponents each time in seven different combat arenas.

Robot Arena £29.99

Every Grand Prix F1 racing circuit

Here's a chance for amateur Schumachers to test their skills behind the wheel in Formula 1 cars racing at Silverstone, Monte Carlo, Monza and all 16 2001 F1 circuits. This famous driving game will test your nerves as you drive Ferrari, Maclaren, Williams and other team cars in qualifying rounds and championship races. Best with a steering wheel.

Grand Prix 4 £34.99

Who Wants To Be A Millionaire 2

Experience the excitement of the phenomenal TV show. Tackle 1,000 challenging new questions posed by Chris Tarrant himself. Can you walk away with a cool virtual Million-pound cheque? Tantalising interruptions from Tarrant and the powerful original music complete this perfect recreation of TV's favourite game show. A winning combination!

Who Wants To Be A Millionaire 2 Was £29.99 Now £19.99 *Save £10*

Virtual Planetarium
Backyard Family Guide
Recreate the night sky above you for the whole family to explore. Simply click on any body for instant details and speed through the cosmos for a view at up to 600,000 magnification. View 1,000,000 stars along with 110 galaxies and rare eclipses, and print out detailed maps of your discoveries. More than you'll ever see with a telescope ... and you won't have to wait for a clear night.

Starry Night Backyard £39.99

Build your own miniature safari park
Starting with wild bush, design your own safari park. Choose miniature herds of elephant, zebra and wildebeest, prides of lions, and the odd hippo. Decorate your park with exotic trees, vegetation and plants, adding lakes, safari huts, paths and roads. Then watch your holiday makers arrive to take tours in this safari classic. Have fun growing your park or just watch and listen to the animals. Includes 2 bonus game classics, Sim Farm and Sim Earth.

Sim Triple Pack £19.99

I can be an animal expert (5-8 years)
Interact with your favourite animals on animal safaris in incredible 3D recreations of the African plains, tropical rainforest, forest and tide pools. Learn about the habitats of elephants, monkeys, snakes, giraffes, rhinos, hippos and many more. There are hours and hours of fun learning here, with 16 action-packed animal adventures, lots of challenges and some fantastic tunes, in your lively journey to become an animal expert. *Early learning at its very best.*

Jump Ahead Frankie Animal Adventures £19.99

Mystery of the Druids
A simple murder turns out to be the climax of a sacred ritual initiated over 1,000 years ago. Visit Stonehenge and Epping Forest, plus mansions and mausoleums and even travel back in time to follow this sinister plot. During your investigation, you'll need to communicate with Scotland Yard, get information out of reluctant witnesses and sort through clues and puzzles. A real thriller, described by PC Zone magazine as 'the best serious adventure game

Mystery of the Druids £29.99

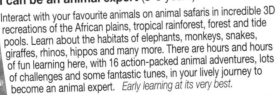

Our Odyssey in the Amazonian jungle – on 4 CDs
Years ago, a sacred bird's egg was stolen from the jungles of Central America, releasing sinister supernatural forces. You – a young journalist intrigued by the story – promise to return the egg to the native Indians. Experience the heat & humidity, exotic wildlife, vegetations, mist, waterfalls ... the graphics are fabulous and the soundtrack deeply atmospheric. Hundreds of locations to explore (on 4 CDs!). Amerzone took three years to produce – the result is remarkable!

Amerzone £29.99

I would choose ....
because ....
....
....

Reviews

2 Eight people looked at the software catalogue and each one chose a different game. Read what they said about it. Which game did each person buy?

Derek

This looks great. I've always been interested in astronomy and this is a great way of learning more. You don't have to own a telescope, and you don't have to stand outside in the cold staring up at the sky.

Derek chose ....

Polly

I went for this one because I thought it sounded fun trying to beat the thief at this own game and get him arrested. It sounds like a real test of skill — getting away after you've taken them. Also I'm quite good at reading maps and finding my way down dark gloomy tunnels.

Polly chose ....

Charlie

The reason I chose this one was because I like quizzes and game shows and anything where I can show off my general knowledge. I've seen the programme on TV and, you know, it gets quite tense and exciting. Also I thought this one was good value for money — I mean, it's been reduced in price quite a bit, hasn't it?

Charlie chose ....

Stephen

This one caught my eye because I'm interested in wildlife and, by coincidence, I want to be a journalist one day. Also, I like the idea of supernatural powers at work. You can tell that a lot of time and skill went into producing this piece of software.

Stephen chose ....

Beth

I'm fascinated by ancient history so this appealed to me straightaway. The time travel idea sounds good and I like the sound of the detective work and the creepy atmosphere. I've tried other murder mysteries but this one looked a bit different.

Beth chose ....

Liam

I wanted this one because I really like designing gadgets and home made machines. I like the combat element in the game, too, and the chance to stop my opponents with all sorts of deadly devices! I like the idea that it's a battle of machines rather than men or monsters.

Liam chose ....

Hannah

I've always been interested in wildlife, African big game in particular. I like the idea of creating an environment for animals — that sounds fun. Also, for no extra cost, you get 2 extra games.

Hannah chose ....

Sam

I love speed and racing and all that stuff. I've tried other driving games but they were too easy for me. I want a challenge! I've got a steering wheel on my console so it seemed just the thing for me.

Sam chose ....

3 Read the reviews again and find the word or phrase in the text which means:

1 the underground canals that carry away dirty water **s** _e_ _w_ _e_ _r_ _s_

2 an occasion when the moon is between the earth and the sun so that for a short time you cannot see part or all of the sun **e** _ _ _ _ _ _

3 confront, for example in battle **f** _ _ _ _ **u** _ **t** _

4 a group of elephants **h** _ _ _ _ a group of lions **p** _ _ _ _

5 the opposite of professional **a** _ _ _ _ _ _ _

6 musical melodies **t** _ _ _ _ _

7 to try to answer **t** _ _ _ _ _

8 the Criminal Investigation Department of the London Metropolitan Police **S** _ _ _ _ _ _ _ _ _ **Y** _ _ _ _

9 fascinated (by something strange) **i** _ _ _ _ _ _ _ _ _

At the library

1 Jackie works in the local library every Saturday. Today she has a big pile of books to put back on the shelves. Look at the titles of the books and put them into the correct category.

Book titles:
- Cool Desserts
- Madame Doubtfire
- A GUIDE TO PROGRAMMING
- What Happens in Parliament
- Teach Yourself E-Commerce
- 100 Greatest Women
- Lives of the Saints
- Confident Cooking
- Life Drawing
- The Snake Book
- An Introduction to Pottery
- Sikhism
- Rough Water Canoeing
- The Oxford Children's Encyclopaedia
- Dr. Jekyll & Mr Hyde
- Naturewatch: Bears & Pandas
- J.K. Rowling: The Wizard Behind Harry Potter
- THE WANDERINGS OF ODYSSEUS
- The Guiness Book of Answers
- The Young Gymnast
- British Folk Tales
- The United Nations
- Gods & Heroes from Viking Mythology

Reference Books
The Oxford Children's Encyclopaedia
....
....

Traditional Tales, Myths and Legends
....
....
....

Arts and Crafts
....
....

Animals
....
....

Sports
....
....

Famous People
....
....

Religions
....
....

Politics and Society
....
....

Food and Drink
....
....

General Fiction
....
....

Computers
....
....

At the library

2 Here are extracts from three of the books Jackie put on the shelf. They are muddled up. Divide them into three separate texts and write the title of the book each one comes from.

a Once upon a time there was an old couple who were very sad because they had no children.

b A rare and closely protected animal, it lives in the cool, damp bamboo forests of mountainous central China.

c Beat the egg whites until stiff.

d 'If only we had even one child to comfort us in our old age!' said the husband.

e Their thick, woolly coat is black or brownish black and yellowish white; the darker color forms patches around the eyes, covers the ears, legs, and chest, and forms a band across the shoulders.

f Remove the blackcurrant mixture from the freezer, beat thoroughly, then fold in the egg whites until evenly blended.

g 'Yes,' said his wife, 'I wouldn't care if the child was no bigger than my own thumb!'

h Bamboo constitutes most of their diet, but they may also feed on other plants and even an occasional small animal.

i Return to the container, cover and freeze for at least 2 hours or until firm.

Book 1

Title ....

Text ....
....
....
....

Book 2

Title ....

Text ....
....
....
....

Book 3

Title ....

Text ....
....
....
....

Blurbs

> **blurb** /blɜ:b/ The blurb about a new book, film, or exhibition is information that is written about it in order to attract people's interest. [INFORMAL]
> *Collins Cobuild English Dictionary*

THE HAUNTING OF ALAIZABEL CRAY

Amongst the dark streets of London, dwells unimaginable terror …

It happened after the Vernichtung – the war left the city damaged, bruised, battered, its people shattered and battle-scarred, and open to a terrifying retribution …

Foul things lurk within the labyrinth of the Old Quarter, and those who venture out at night are easy prey. Prey for the wolves and murderers that stalk the crooked streets, and for creatures far more deadly – the wych-kin.

But evil disguised is deadliest of all. And behind the façade of wealth and charity that surrounds the uppermost levels of society lies a terrifying pact with the wych-kin that threatens humankind's very existence.

At its heart is the beautiful, vulnerable, enigmatic Alaizabel Cray – key to the ultimate evil.

Chris Wooding weaves an utterly compelling story set against a vividly imagined cityscape. You will be drawn irresistibly into its cobbled lanes, where the darkness awaits.

BLOOD SINISTER

A TALE TO MAKE YOUR BLOOD RUN COLD …

The old, leather-bound diary is just a diversion for Ellen Forrest at first. Sent to rest at her grandmother's house, she begins reading to take her mind off her mysterious illness. For no one knows why she's so pale and drawn, so bloodless

But the bizarre history that unfolds is so compelling, so strangely tangled up with her own life, that reading proves impossible. Ellen begins to feel even more drained than before... Could something be reaching across the centuries to claim her, bleeding her dry...?

footloose
it's the only way to be

Going on holiday with your boyfriend should be heavenly; spending all that time together, fooling around in the sun – bliss. So when he says he wants you to go camping with him and four of his mates, what do you do?

You leave him behind.

When Kelly arrives in Greece with Jade and Sarah, she knows she's done the right thing. The clifftop farmhouse is gorgeous, the sea and sun are fantastic and the freedom makes her dizzy. The days stretch out idyllically before the three girls, and the nights … It couldn't be more perfect, until a van arrives with five familiar lads in it …

PLEX

'The creature you have just liberated will be very agile. Long arms. Good eyes. Considerable intelligence. Plus …' He glances at us. 'Aggressive instincts and sharp teeth.'

Todd is different from the others. He's supposed to be into sports and trainers and hanging around with friends, not sitting alone, thinking about *monsters* …

Then Todd meets Sly, and they become friends because they are both outsiders. Together they discover **Mr Multiplex**, a man with the unusual gift of plexing – the ability to mix two things together to make what he calls 'the best of both worlds'.

But Mr Multiplex has just plexed a dog with a gibbon, and frightening result – a 'gog' has escaped …

Will they manage to find the missing creature before *it* finds them?

Shaunna isn't fussy – much. She's just not going to settle for an ordinary guy like her sister's gone and done. Ruth's got this cutesy white wedding planned, but Shaunna can't imagine anything more soul-destroying than a life with Boring Brian. and as for the apricot meringue of a bridesmaid's dress that Ruth is guilt-tripping her into …

Stuff **red roses** and corny romance – Shauna wants a sweet soulmate who'll drape daisy chains around her neck. But is the boy of her daydreams out there anywhere?

Blurbs

1 **Read the five book blurbs and answer these questions.**

Which book …

1 is about three girls on holiday together? ....

2 is about evil forces at work in high society? ....

3 is about two boys who meet an inventor? ....

4 is about a girl who is going to be a bridesmaid? ....

5 is about a girl reading an old diary? ....

2 **Write the names in the gaps.**

1 .... is looking for a boyfriend who will really understand her.

2 .... is taking a rest cure for a mystery illness.

3 .... are the most dangerous creatures on the streets of London.

4 .... doesn't want to spend her holiday with a load of boys.

5 .... is a kind of inventor.

6 .... is a mysterious and perhaps dangerous woman.

3 **Which novel would you recommend to:**

1 Inger, who likes stories about vampires. ....

2 Maxine, who adores comedy and romantic fiction. ....

3 Julie, who loves stories set in foreign countries. ....

4 Steve, who likes futuristic stories and horror fiction. ....

5 Rajeev, who often reads stories about monsters. ....

4 **Look at these extracts from the five blurbs & match the underlined words with the correct definitions in the box on the right.**

1 '… a van arrives with five familiar <u>lads</u> in it.' ◯

2 'Shauna isn't <u>fussy</u> – much.' ◯

3 'She begins reading to <u>take her mind off</u> her mysterious illness.' ◯

4 '… a terrifying <u>pact</u> that threatens humankind's very existence' ◯

5 'the creature you have just liberated will be very <u>agile</u>.' ◯

a an agreement between people or organisations to help each other

b can move very quickly and easily

c difficult to please

d boys, or young men

e forget

5 **Which of the five books would you choose to read? Explain in one or two sentences the reasons for your choice.**

....

....

....

Blurbs

6 Below is the cover illustration for a story. Think of a title for the story. Write the blurb to go on the book jacket. When you have finished, read other students' blurbs.

....

....

....

....

....

....

....

....

....

....

....

....

....

Vocabulary

1 Look at the wordsearch. Find the words to match the pictures. Write the correct word next to each picture.

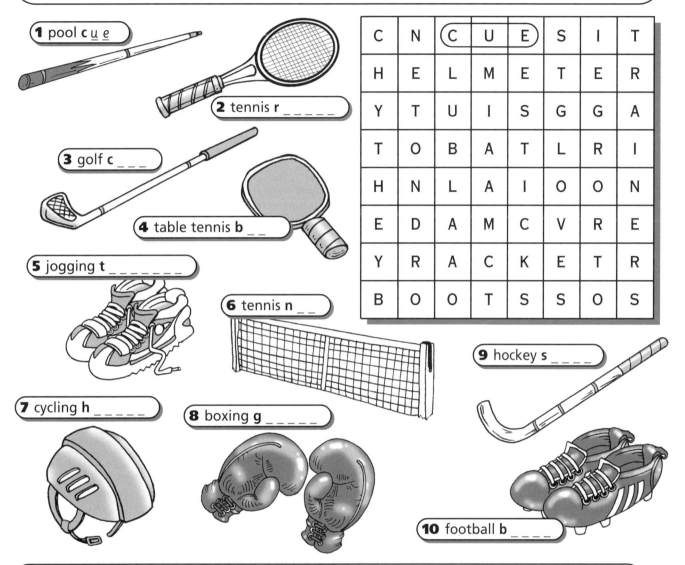

1 pool c u e

2 tennis r _ _ _ _ _

3 golf c _ _ _

4 table tennis b _ _

5 jogging t _ _ _ _ _ _ _

6 tennis n _ _

7 cycling h _ _ _ _ _

8 boxing g _ _ _ _ _

9 hockey s _ _ _ _

10 football b _ _ _ _

C	N	C	U	E	S	I	T
H	E	L	M	E	T	E	R
Y	T	U	I	S	G	G	A
T	O	B	A	T	L	R	I
H	N	L	A	I	O	O	N
E	D	A	M	C	V	R	E
Y	R	A	C	K	E	T	R
B	O	O	T	S	S	O	S

2 <u>Underline</u> the correct words in these sentences.

1 Real Madrid **played** / **won** / **beat** the Champions **List** / **Table** / **League** in 2002.

2 I **played** / **won** / **lost** Daniel **in** / **at** / **for** tennis for an hour last night but he is better than me so I **lost** / **beat** / **won** by six **rounds** / **goals** / **games** to four.

3 They are the best **group** / **equipment** / **team** in the **list** / **table** / **league** so they always **beat** / **win** / **lose** when we **win** / **play** / **lose** them **in** / **at** / **for** football.

4 I can't **play** / **make** / **do** golf very well so I never **beat** / **make** / **win**.

5 Our volleyball **group** / **equipment** / **team** is getting stronger and we are **beating** / **winning** / **losing** more **groups** / **equipments** / **teams** than before.

6 In our last football **set** / **round** / **match** we **kicked** / **scored** / **did** five **goals** / **scores** / **hits**.

Sports reports

1 Look at these sentences from reports of different sports. Match each sentence to the correct picture.

a

c

e

g

i

j

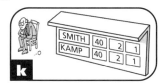

k

1 It was a one-all draw. ..h..

2 Anna was forty love up in the sixth game. ....

3 She holed a three-metre putt on the eighteenth. ....

4 Macaroni led from the first lap to the last. ....

5 He finished with a round of 72. ....

6 The second set went to a tie-break. ....

7 Trueman scored a magnificent try. ....

8 The final game finished 21-18. ....

9 The final score was one-nil. ....

10 Serena served an ace. ....

11 McDonald converted the try. ....

12 He scored a strike. ....

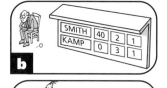

b

d

f

h

l

2 Look at these football results. Write answers to the questions.

Arsenal 2 (1)
Henry 26, Kanu 90
Bolton 1 (0)
Farrelly 47
Kanu's late winner gave Arsenal an eleventh consecutive home league win, equalling a club record.
Thierry Henry has scored five goals and set up four more so far this season.

Liverpool 1 (0)
Owen 56
West Ham 1 (1)
Kanoute 13
Owen ended this season's goal drought with a superb second half strike from 25 feet.
West Ham started well but couldn't resist Liverpool pressure.

Manchester United 1 (0)
Van Nistelroy 63 pen
Aston Villa 0 (0)
A disputed penalty settled this uninspiring display when Van Nistelroy made no mistake from the spot.
Villa still haven't had a win under their new manager.

1 Which match ended in a one-all draw?
Liverpool v West Ham

2 At Liverpool, which team was winning at half time?
....

3 Was it a good match at Manchester United? ....

4 How many times has Henry scored a goal this season? ....

5 Has Owen scored many goals this season? ....

6 What record did Kanu's goal give Arsenal?
....

7 Did West Ham play better in the first half or the second half? ....

8 Did everyone agree that it was a clear penalty at Manchester United? ....

9 How many times has Aston Villa won since changing their manager? ....

League table

1 Complete the league table with all the missing figures. The information and questions below will help you.

		HOME					AWAY						
	P	W	D	L	F	A	W	D	L	F	A	GD	Pts
1 Arsenal	7	◯	◯	◯	11	4	◯	2	0	6	3	10	17
2 Liverpool	7	2	2	0	9	4	2	1	0	6	4	◯	15
3 Man Utd	7	3	◯	◯	6	3	◯	◯	◯	5	6	2	13
4 Leeds	6	2	0	1	4	1	2	0	1	6	3	6	◯
5 Chelsea	6	1	2	◯	6	◯	2	1	◯	7	5	5	12
17 Man City	6	1	0	◯	4	5	1	0	◯	3	6	-4	6
18 Aston Villa	7	1	3	0	2	1	0	0	3	◯	6	-4	6
19 Bolton	◯	0	1	2	1	5	1	1	2	1	5	-8	5
20 West Ham	6	◯	◯	◯	2	5	0	0	2	2	7	-8	2

P = played
L = lost
W = won
F = goals for
D = drawn
A = goals against
GD = goal difference
Pts = points
(win = 3 points,
draw = 1 points)
Man Utd =
Manchester United
Man City =
Manchester City

1 The team which is top of the league has won four games at home and one game away.

2 The team which is bottom of the league has drawn two games and lost two games at home.

3 How many games has the team which is second from bottom played? ....

4 What's the goal difference of the team that's second from the top? ....

5 Which three teams are unbeaten so far this season? ....

6 The third-placed team has won one game and drawn one game away.

7 How many points has the fourth-placed team got? ....

8 How many goals has Aston Villa scored away from home? ....

9 How many games has Manchester City lost? ....

10 How many goals have been scored against Chelsea at home? ....

Lyrics

1 Look at the verse 1 of Song A. Then use the words in the box to complete verse 2.

Song A   friend heart falling feeling phone calling

Baby, silly for me to feel this way
about you and her,
Cos' I know she's been such a good friend
I know she has helped you through.

Talking late on the ⬭
Every night you've been ⬭
Private moments alone
And your heart soon be ⬭

And I know she's a ⬭
But I can't shake the ⬭
That I could be losing your ⬭

2 Match the sentence halves to make verse 3.

You said	you're in love with me
How deep	were not to get in between
And intentions	I see possibilities
But	that she's done well to see

3 Use the correct form of these verbs to complete verse 4: *feel, see, enjoy, know.*

And you say that you feel

I'm the best thing in your life

And I ⬭ it's real, ⬭ it in your eyes

There's no reason for me, to even

⬭ this way

I know you just ⬭ her company

4 Look at these two choruses. Which one is the correct chorus for Song A?

I think I'm jealous of your girlfriend
Although she's just a girl that is your friend
I think I'm jealous of your girlfriend
She shares a special part of you

Chorus 1

I don't want to run away but I can't
take it I don't understand
If I'm not made for you then why
does my heart tell me that I am?
Is there any way that I can stay in your arms?

Chorus 2

5 Look at these two song titles. Which one is the correct song title for Song A?

Girlfriend

If you're not the one

Lyrics

6 Now look at Song B. Match the sentence halves to make verse 1.

Song B

If you're not the one, then why does my soul

If you're not the one, then why does my hand

If you are not mine, then why does your heart

If you are not mine, would I have the strength

return my call?

feel glad today?

to stand at all?

fit yours this way?

I never know what the future brings
but I know you are here with me now.
We'll make it through and I hope
You are the one I share my life with

7 Use the correct form of these verbs to complete verse 2: *do (not), is.*

If I ⟨　　⟩ need you, then why ⟨　　⟩ I crying on my bed?

If I ⟨　　⟩ need you, then why ⟨　　⟩ your name resound in my head?

If you ⟨　　⟩ not for me, then why ⟨　　⟩ this distance maim my life?

If you ⟨　　⟩ not for me, then why ⟨　　⟩ I dream of you as my wife?

8 Use the letters to complete the words for verse 3.

I don't know why you're so far away

But I know that this much is (t)○○○○

We'll make it through and I hope

You are the one I (s)○○○○○ my life with

And I wish that you could be the one I (d)○○ with

And I'm praying you're the one I (b)○○○○○ my home with

I hope I (l)○○○○ you all my life

i **v** **r**
a **h** **u**
i **d** **u**
e **e**
e **o** **r**
e **l**

9 Use the prepositions to complete verse 4: *with, by, for, away, to, into.*

Cos I miss you

Body and soul so strong that

it takes my breath ⟨　　⟩

And I breathe you ⟨　　⟩ my heart

and pray ⟨　　⟩ the strength ⟨　　⟩ stand today.

Cos I love you

Whether it's wrong or right and

though I can't be ⟨　　⟩ you tonight

And though my heart is ⟨　　⟩ your side.

At the museum

1 Look at these signs for various different services and facilities in a museum. Use the words in the box to label each sign.

Disabled toilet   Audio tour   Ticket desk
Shop   Babycare   Café   Lost property   First Aid
Toilets
Restaurant   Cloakroom   Information Desk

1 information desk

2

3

4

5

6

7

8

9

10

11

12

2 Listen to these 7 short conversations. Where does each conversation take place?

1

2

3

4

5

6

7

At the museum

3 Museum Fun! Look at this list of some of the many museums, galleries and exhibits in London. Then read and match the descriptions below to the correct museum.

Imperial War Museum, ⊖ Elephant & Castle

London Dungeon, Tooley Street, SE1, ⊖ London Bridge

London Museums of Health & Medicine

London Transport Museum, ⊖ Covent Garden

Madame Tussaud's Waxworks, ⊖ Baker Street

Museum of London - *The history of the capital city from the earliest times*, Barbican

National Gallery - *The nation's finest collection of European paintings*, Charing Cross

National Maritime Museum, Greenwich

Science Museum, ⊖ South Kensington

Shakespeare's Globe Exhibition & Theatre, ⊖ Mansion House

Sherlock Holmes Museum, 221B Baker Street, ⊖ Baker Street

Tower of London - *Once a notorious prison, now home to the crown jewels of the British monarchy*, ⊖ Tower Hill

Tower Bridge Experience, ⊖ Tower Hill

Victoria & Albert Museum - *A great collection of applied arts (ceramics, metalwork, furniture, fashion)* ⊖ South Kensington

1 See how the Victorians travelled! Drive a Tube simulator! It's trams, trains, buses and much more. A truly memorable, hands-on, moving experience!

London Transport Museum

2 You can look out across London from this unique vantage point and witness the rich history and bold engineering invention that made it one of the most famous landmarks in the world.

3 Who would you like a close encounter with? Kylie Minogue, Michael Jackson, Princess Diana, Nelson Mandela? They, and thousands of other famous figures, are all here.

4 Step back in time and visit London's most famous address where (according to his creator, Sir Arthur Conan Doyle), the great detective shared rooms with his assistant, Dr. Watson.

5 The world's greatest museum of seafaring. Themes explored include: 'The Future of the Sea', 'Nelson: Britain's Greatest Admiral', and 'Great Explorers'. You can also visit the Cutty Sark (1869), the only surviving tea ship and one of the fastest merchant sailing vessels ever built.

6 We cover all aspects of life in wartime — heroes, villains, and the millions who are neither — and all human experience, at home and on the battlefield.

7 Deep in the heart of London, buried beneath the pavements of historic Southwark, lies the world's most chillingly famous horror attraction. It brings more than 2000 years of gruesome history back to life ... and death!

8 A faithful reconstruction of the site where his famous plays were performed, together with an exhibition of the development of that spectacular period in British and world drama.

9 Visit the stunning Whiteleys Silver Galleries: outstanding silver treasures from 1400 to the present day.

10 On the second floor you can find exhibitions on Chemistry in Everyday Life, Printing and Papermaking, and Nuclear Energy.

Hampton Court and Leeds Castle

Hampton Court

Leeds Castle

500 years of royal history. Hampton Court has been home to many of Britain's most famous kings and queens. With its wonderful state apartments and beautiful formal gardens, it promises you a magical history tour.

It's been called 'The loveliest castle in the world.' As you come out of the surrounding woods it stands before you in a breath-taking setting — the castle of your dreams.

1 Match the definitions below.

1 Leather band put around a dog's neck.		**moat**
2 Grapes grow on this plant.		**costume**
3 This is like a labyrinth so you can easily get lost in it.		**dog collar**
4 This is like a large cage and birds are kept in it.		**vine**
5 This means clothes of a certain historical period.		**aviary**
6 A channel filled with water, all around a castle, to keep people out!		**peacock**
7 This means to walk slowly, with no special destination in mind.		**maze**
8 The name of a flightless bird with a beautiful plumed tail.		**wander**

2 🎧 Look at the table below. You can find some of these attractions at Hampton Court, some at Leeds Castle and some at both places. Listen to Peter, a tour guide, and complete the table with ticks (✔).

	HAMPTON COURT	LEEDS CASTLE
royal connections	✔	✔
built in the 11th century		✔
Henry VIII lived there		
beautiful rooms you can visit		
beautiful gardens		
walks along the river		
a maze		
shops		
places to eat and drink		
Tudor kitchens		
an aviary		
a very old vine		
a golf course		
an unusual museum		
lakes and a moat		
tours with guides in costume		
a fine collection of paintings		
a Shakespeare play in the summer		

Text messages

1 Laura loves texting messages to her best friend Rachael. When she texts, Laura makes her words as short as possible. These are some of the letters she uses instead of words. Spell the word she wants to say in the space.

1 @   I'll meet you <u>a</u> <u>t</u> 11.00.

2 b   I may __ __ late.

3 c   Let's __ __ __ a film tonight.

4 gtg   I've __ __ __ __ __ __ now.

5 n   fish __ __ __ chips

6 r   __ __ __ you happy?

7 T   I'll wear jeans and a __ - __ __ __ __ __ __ .

8 u   Where do __ __ __ live?

9 y   __ __ __ did you phone me?

2 Laura often uses the numbers: 1, 2 and 8 to make words shorter when she texts. Write the missing number to complete the word. The clues will help you. Then write the correct spelling of the word in the gap.

		CLUES	
1	L 8	(not early)	L A T E
2	G R __	(very good)	G R __ __ __
3	__ M O R O	(the day after today)	__ __ M O R __ O W
4	S K __ I N	(a sport activity)	S K __ __ I N __
5	__ N I T E	(later today	__ __ N I __ __ T
6	S U M __	(a person)	S __ M __ __ __ __
7	M __	(a friend)	M __ __ __
8	D __	(a time to meet)	D __ __ __

Text messages

3 Laura uses lots of special spellings to save space when she texts. Match the word in A with its correct meaning in B.

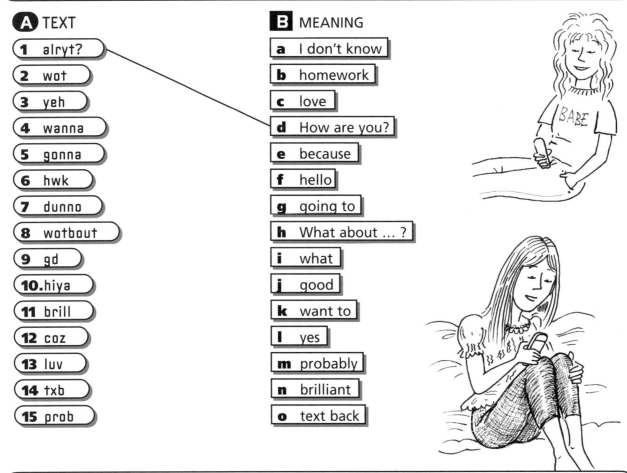

A TEXT

1. alryt?
2. wot
3. yeh
4. wanna
5. gonna
6. hwk
7. dunno
8. wotbout
9. gd
10. hiya
11. brill
12. coz
13. luv
14. txb
15. prob

B MEANING

a I don't know
b homework
c love
d How are you?
e because
f hello
g going to
h What about ... ?
i what
j good
k want to
l yes
m probably
n brilliant
o text back

4 Laura texts Rachael. What do they say? Write the missing words in the gaps to complete their full conversations.

1 Hiya! alryt? wot u dun 2day? wanna meet @ 11? txb

Hello, h o w are y o u ? _ _ _ _ _ are _ _ _ _ _ _ _ _ _
today? Do _ _ _ _ _ _ _ _ to meet _ _ 11 o'clock? _ _ _ _ _
back.

2 OK. wot u wanna do? wot u gonna wear?

OK. _ _ _ _ _ do _ _ _ _ want _ _ do? _ _ _ _ _ are
you _ _ _ _ _ _ to wear?

3 Meet in town n shop. gonna wear jeans n a T.

Meet in town _ _ _ shop. I'm _ _ _ _ _ _ to wear
jeans _ _ _ a _ - _ _ _ _ _ .

Conversations

1 In the town today there are lots of people having conversations on their mobile phones. Who is speaking to whom? Draw a line to make pairs.

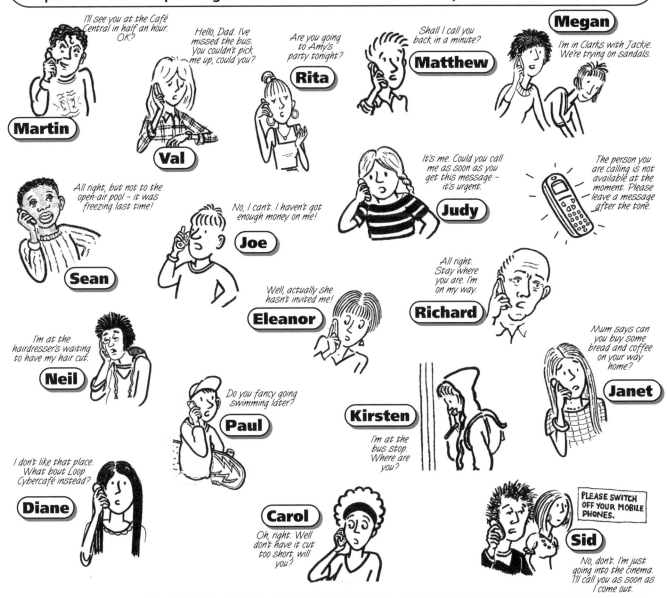

2 One person is left with no speaking partner. Who is it? ....

3 Now write the name of the correct person in the space.

1 .... doesn't like cold water.

2 .... is going to give his daughter a lift in the car.

3 .... hasn't been asked to the party.

4 .... is going to switch his mobile off.

5 .... is in a shoe shop.

6 .... suggests a different place to meet.

7 .... is passing on a request from her mother.

8 .... gets an automatic answering service.

9 .... is at the hairdresser's.

Conversations

1 Read the responses in pictures 1- 12. What do you think the other person is saying? Listen to the recording and check your answers. Write the correct sentence in the speech bubbles below.

2 Practise the conversations with a partner.

3 Memory Check! Listen to the sentences again. Reply with the correct response without looking at this worksheet!

Messages

1 People in Britain send a lot of greetings cards. There are cards for many different events and occasions. Look at these greetings cards and match them to the occasions in the box. Label the cards.

1 retirement

2

3

4

5

6

7

25 Years

8

Thank You!

9

10

- Christmas
- the birth of a baby
- to thank someone
- moving to a new home
- retiring
- a birthday
- a wedding anniversary
- Valentine's Day
- getting married
- Mother's Day

Messages

---

2 Here are the greetings to write inside the cards, but the words are jumbled up. Put the words in the right order then match the greeting with the correct card.

a happiness both you in the good wishing and luck future
Wishing you both happiness and good luck in the future .... card 3 ....

b new a Christmas merry and year happy
....

c luck your home in good new
....

d your of daughter on the congratulations baby birth
....

e admirer love a from with secret
....

f best world the in the mum to
....

g happy the of day returns many
....

h healthy a wishing retirement and you happy
....

i generous lot for thanks a gift the
....

j anniversary your silver wishes best on wedding
....

---

3 People often write a special personal message inside a greetings card. Match these personal messages to the right card.

① 6

With lots of love from a devoted daughter.

②

I never thought you'd tie the knot!

③

Can't wait to see the little 'bundle of joy'!

④

GUESS WHO?

⑤

With all your hobbies and interests I'm sure you'll still find plenty to do!

⑥

Your new place sounds lovely. I'm looking forward to seeing it once you've settled in.

⑦

From today you can vote, get married, borrow money from the bank, drink alcohol in a pub and... go to prison!

⑧

The earrings are beautiful and go really well with my new dress.

⑨

25 years together without a single quarrel ~ an example to all of us!

⑩

Let's try and meet up in the new year.

Announcements and signs

1 Unscramble the words to describe the pictures.

1 rigaecra c.................

or choca c ....

2 flortpam p.................

3 refa f........

4 agrud g........

5 stainedotin d.................

6 tomprecanmt c.................

7 ekictt irberar t............ b ....

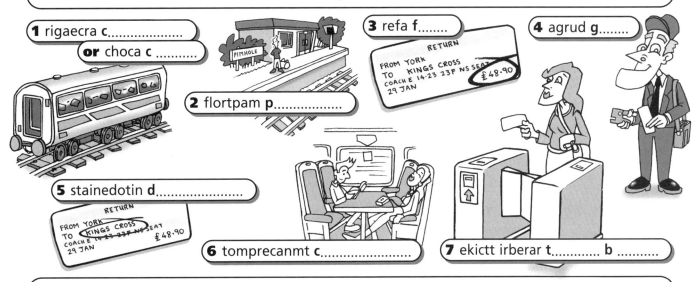

2 Match the two parts of these sentences to make the correct train announcements.

1 This is the London Victoria train. Calling ⓓ

2 I'm very sorry ◯

3 This is Hove. Change here ◯

4 Customers for Portsmouth must travel ◯

5 Customers are reminded ◯

6 Any more tickets ◯

7 This train is formed ◯

8 Platform ◯

9 Do not open the doors ◯

10 Please ensure ◯

a in the front four carriages.

b two for the Birmingham New Street service.

c for inspection, please?

d at Gatwick airport and East Croydon.

e until the train has come to a complete stop.

f you travel in the correct part of the train.

g not to leave luggage unattended.

h for the delay to this service.

i of four coaches.

j for the Brighton service.

3 Where would you see these signs and warnings? Write the number of the correct warning next to each sign.

1 Alarm. Pull the chain. Penalty for improper use £50. ⓑ

2 Passengers must not cross the line. ◯

3 Do not alight here. ◯

4 No smoking. Penalty £50 maximum. ◯

5 Danger. Do not touch the live rail. ◯

6 Danger. Do not lean out of the window or open the door when the train is moving. ◯

Vocabulary and fares

1 <u>Underline</u> the correct words in these sentences.

1 It's too far to walk. We need to **have / catch / ride** a bus to the station.

2 There's a long **line / file / queue** waiting for the bus.

3 Get **off / down / from** the bus at the next **stand / stop / halt**.

4 Oh dear! The bus has just gone. We've **missed / lost / left** it.

5 I haven't got enough money for my bus **price / cost / fare**.

6 In London many buses have a **controller / conductor / ticket-taker** as well as a driver.

7 I don't think the cinema is on this bus **route / road / way** - you need a number 15.

8 My bus **journey / travel / trip** usually takes about twenty minutes.

9 'All buses are designated No **Fuming / Smoking / Firing** Areas.'

2 Look at this information about bus fares. Then write your answers to the questions.

Fares and conditions

Period of Travel	Cost	Where to buy
One journey	£1	buy on bus
One day *(unlimited journeys anywhere)*	£2.60 SAVER	buy on bus or £2.50 in advance
One day central *(unlimited journeys central area)*	£2.20 CENTRESAVER	buy on bus
One week *(any 7 consecutive days)*	£13 SAVER	buy in advance - also 4-pack for £42
One month *(fixed calendar month)*	£42 SAVER	buy in advance

■ **Special Senior Deals** Buy a Countycard for half price travel for one journey.
■ **Special Junior Deals** Get a Bus ID (ages 5-16) or Bus ID+ (ages 16-18) for fares of:
10p accompanied (by one adult)
30p solo (weekends & after 6pm on schooldays)
£1.30 - 1 day SAVER
£6 - 1 week SAVER
£20 - 1 month SAVER

■ **Special Student Deals** Student card holders get special deals on 1 week SAVER tickets and pay just £30 for a 1 month SAVER ticket
■ **Buy In Advance** SAVER 1 day, 1 week and 1 month tickets are available from all Post Offices and many newsagents.
■ **Return Journey For £1** Local return journeys are available for £1 in residential areas. *See list on next page for details*

■ **Travelling Afar** Explorer SAVERs are available offering great value. *See list on page 13 for details.*
■ **Exceptions** SAVER tickets are not valid on Park & Ride, or Night Buses.
£1 flat fare tickets are only available on the designated routes.

1 Where can you buy a one month SAVER ticket? ....

2 If you are a student, what's the cheapest price of a one month SAVER ticket? ....

3 Can you use a SAVER ticket on a night bus? ....

4 If you live near the centre of the town, how much do you have to pay for a journey into the town and then back home again? ....

5 Do you have to pay the full adult fare if you are 17 years old? ....

6 If you are thirteen years old, how much does one month's bus travel cost? ....

7 How much do you save if you buy a one day ticket in advance? ....

8 If you want to travel out of town by bus, what kind of ticket should you ask for? ....

Timetables

1 Look at this bus timetable and then answer the questions.

	a.m.	a.m.	a.m.	then at these minutes past each hour until			p.m.	p.m.	p.m.	p.m.	p.m.
Brighton Univ.	8.25	◯	9.25	55	25		◯	6.55	◯	◯	◯
Lewes Road	8.28	8.58	◯	58	◯		5.58	◯	◯	◯	◯
Open Market	◯	9.03	9.33	33	◯		6.03	◯	8.03	◯	
Old Steine	◯	◯	9.38	◯	◯		◯	◯		9.08	◯
Brighton Stn	◯	9.13	◯	13	◯		◯	7.13	◯	◯	10.13

1 Write in all the missing times.

2 What's the difference between a.m. and p.m.? ....

3 How long does it take to go from Brighton University to Brighton Station? ....

4 Laura lives near Brighton University. She must catch a train to London at 3.30 pm.
   What time is her bus? ....

5 Jamie is at Lewes Road. It's 7.15 pm. How long must he wait till his next bus? ....

6 What time does the last bus leave Brighton University? ....

2 Look at these clocks and watches. Where is the bus at these times?

Instructions

1 🎧 Here are some instructions you can see and hear on a bus. One word is missing from each sentence. Look at the wordsearch and find the missing word. Then listen to check your answers.

1 .... TIGHT PLEASE!

2 Please do not .... to the driver.

3 Press to .... the bell.

4 PASSENGERS ARE NOT ALLOWED TO .... BEYOND THIS POINT.

5 No .... given.

6 Any more .... please!

7 PLEASE .... ALL CIGARETTES.

8 .... up this seat to a disabled person.

B	E	S	G	U	E	K	R	E	C
E	X	T	I	N	G	U	I	S	H
A	T	O	V	A	R	S	N	T	O
F	A	R	E	S	E	P	G	A	L
T	C	H	A	N	G	E	I	N	D
O	H	I	N	A	I	A	N	D	I
L	E	T	D	Y	D	K	G	E	M

2 Write three good things and three bad things about travelling by bus. Then compare your ideas with a friend.

	Good things	**Bad things**
1	....	....
	....	....
2	....	....
	....	....
3	....	....
	....	....

Announcements and notices

1 Using the words in the box, label the pictures.

boarding gate · boarding pass · aisle seat · check-in desk · excess baggage · customs · baggage reclaim · passenger · luggage · hand luggage

1

2

3

4

5

6

7

8 boarding gate

9

10

2 Listen to these announcements and conversations at Gatwick Airport near London. Write the missing information onto the Departures Board.

Flight	No.	Time	Destination	Information	Gate
EasyJet	7732	12.15	Brussels	Delayed – listen to announcements	–
Ryanair	325	12.25	Dublin	Final call	39
Swissair			Geneva		
Alitalia					
			Prague		
Iberian		13.05		Now boarding	
				Go to Airport Information	–
				Delayed to 14.30	–
	4022				–

Announcements and notices

3 Read the airport notice and answer these questions.

1 You mustn't have any of these items with you.

   a when you arrive at the airport check-in ○

   b after you go through passport control ○

   c at any time ○

2 Where should you put these items?

   a In your hand luggage. ○

   b In your suitcase. ○

   c You shouldn't carry these items at all. ○

4 Now match these pictures to the things in the notice. Write the number of each picture next to the correct item in the notice.

IMPORTANT SECURITY INFORMATION

You are now prohibited from carrying certain items into the departure area after security search. If you have any of the items listed below please place them in baggage to be checked in.

Prohibited Items
The following list is not exhaustive:

Toy or replica guns ③
○ Catapults / slingshots
Knitting needles ○
○ Sports bats / clubs / cues
Darts ○
○ Tools
Razor blades ○
○ Hypodermic syringes
Knives ○
○ Cutlery
Scissors ○

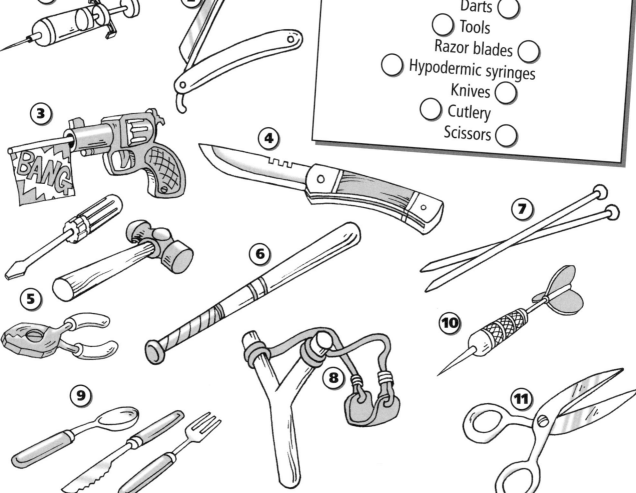

Check-in

1 🎧 **Jane is travelling from Gatwick, near London, to Rome. Listen to her conversation at the check-in desk. There are fourteen mistakes in the script. Find the mistakes and correct them.**

Jane:	Good morning.
Ground staff:	Hello, can I see your ticket and passport, please? Is it just one briefcase you have?
Jane:	Yes, and two bits of hand luggage.
Ground staff:	OK, can you just lift it onto the desk? Did you make your suitcase yourself?
Jane:	Yes.
Ground staff:	Have you got any technical or flammable items in your case?
Jane:	No, I've got a walkman, razor and my phone with me here.
Ground staff:	That's OK. Look at this list. Are you carrying any of the items in your hand luggage?
Jane:	No, my things are in the case.
Ground staff:	Good. Have you left your case unattached at any time since you packed it?
Jane:	No.
Ground staff:	OK, that's fine. Would you prefer a window seat or I'll sit?
Jane:	I think a window seat, please.
Ground staff:	OK, here's your board and pass with your seat number. It'll be Gate 25. If you go through secrets and passport control you can wait in the departure lunch … or have a look at the shops while you're waiting. Make sure you look at the screams to see when your flight starts boring. Have a good flight!
Jane:	Thanks.

2 Now work with a friend and read the dialogue aloud.

3 Look at the information on Jane's ticket and answer the questions below.

1 What time should Jane check in?

  a at about 9.45 ◯

  b at about 11.15 ◯

  c at about 11.25 ◯

2 How long does the flight take?

  a fifty minutes ◯

  b one hour and fifty minutes ◯

  c two hours and fifty minutes ◯

3 Where must she be 20 minutes before she gets on the plane?

  a at check-in ◯

  b at passport control ◯

  c at the boarding gate ◯

4 Write in full the day and date of her flights ....

5 What must Jane remember to take with her?..

6 Jane has got a suitcase weighing 25 kilos, a plastic carrier bag full of gifts and a large leather handbag. What do you think the check-in assistant will say?..

Air Olympia

IMPORTANT REMINDERS
Check-in 2 hours prior to scheduled departure.
Check-in closes 30 minutes prior to departure.
You must be at the boarding gate 20 minutes prior to departure.
It is advisable for passengers who book in advance to reconfirm their outward/return flights at least 24 hours prior to departure.
Checked baggage allowance is 20kg., any excess over 20kg is chargeable at an excess rate per kilo.
Only one piece of hand luggage, not more than 5 kgs, is allowed in the cabin.
Valid passport required for international services.

Air Olympia

OUTWARD
From Gatwick (GWK) to Rome (ROM)
Sat, 13Apr Flight BA822 Depart GWK at 11:45
and arrive ROM at 12:35

INWARD
From Rome (ROM) to Gatwick (GWK)
Sat, 20Apr Flight BA823 Depart ROM at 13.50
and arrive GWK at 16:40

PASSENGERS
1 JANE STRONG

Places in Britain

1 Last summer, Tomas and Emilia had a holiday in Britain. They went to ten different places. Listen to the recording and draw a line on the map showing their journey.

Places in Britain

2 Now test your memory. Don't look at the map!

1 The name of a beautiful national park in North Wales.

2 An old university town 100 km from London.

3 The town where Shakespeare was born.

4 In this city by the sea there's a royal palace and a pier.

5 A place where you can see 2nd World War fighter planes.

6 The town associated with Robin Hood.

7 An island off the west coast of Scotland.

8 Where are Princes Street and the Royal Mile?

9 This northern English city is good if you are interested in trains.

10 An area of great natural beauty linked with the names of two famous poets.

3 Look at the map again and find the following:

1 A river in the north-east of England.

2 A city on the north-east coast of Scotland.

3 A city on the south-west coast of England.

4 A big city about 45 kilometres north of Stratford-upon-Avon.

5 A port on the north-west coast of England.

6 The name of the river on which this port lies.

7 An island in the Irish sea.

8 An area of north-west England famous for its mountains and lakes.

9 The name given to the mountainous area of northern Scotland.

10 A historic city in the south east corner of England.

11 A famous university town in central east England.

12 A city in the south of Wales (also its capital).

Travel tips

1 The London underground railway is called *the tube*. Look at this tube information for visitors to London. Choose one word from the box to complete each tip. Sometimes the word is repeated in the tip.

yellow line	platforms	backpack
passengers	luggage	underground
rush hours	escalators	air conditioning

1 Please do not bring more .... than you can safely carry. Unlike mainline railways, the tube does not have porters. Our staff are trained to help you but carrying excess .... is not one of their duties.

2 If you are travelling with a .... - take it off and stand it on the floor of the carriage. This takes up less room.

3 The tube can get very busy, especially during the morning and evening .... Avoid travelling at those times if possible.

4 Londoners stand on the right on the .... at all times. This allows those in a hurry to get past.

5 Please stand to one side of walkways and .... when looking at maps. You are on holiday but the locals are still working and again, always in a hurry. Better still, ask our staff for directions.

Getting around:

Tips for visitors - how to act like a local

6 Please allow .... off the train before you board. This is not the British being polite but it is the safest and quickest way for a train to unload and load ....

7 Please stand behind the .... on platforms. This is for your safety as trains pull in and out.

8 The tube can get very hot during the summer months. It does not yet have .... Please carry lots of water during hot weather.

9 Most importantly, enjoy our city and our railway! The tube is the oldest .... in the world and is an attraction all on its own. It will take you to all the places in London you will ever want to see.

2 Write the number of the tip or tips which give advice about:

a suitcases — tip 1

b travelling between 7.30 and 9.00 am & 5.00 and 6.30 pm. ....

c moving staircases ....

d waiting for trains ....

e getting on trains ....

f blocking the way ....

g having a good time in the city ....

h young people who have a lot of equipment with them ....

3 Write the word or phrase from the tips which means the same as:

a get on a train, plane, bus or ship — board

b have no time ....

c have with you in a pocket or bag ....

d a train which arrives or leaves ....

e by itself ....

f one section of a train ....

g walk to the other side of something ....

h not to do something ....

i people whose job is to carry things for other people ....

Getting around

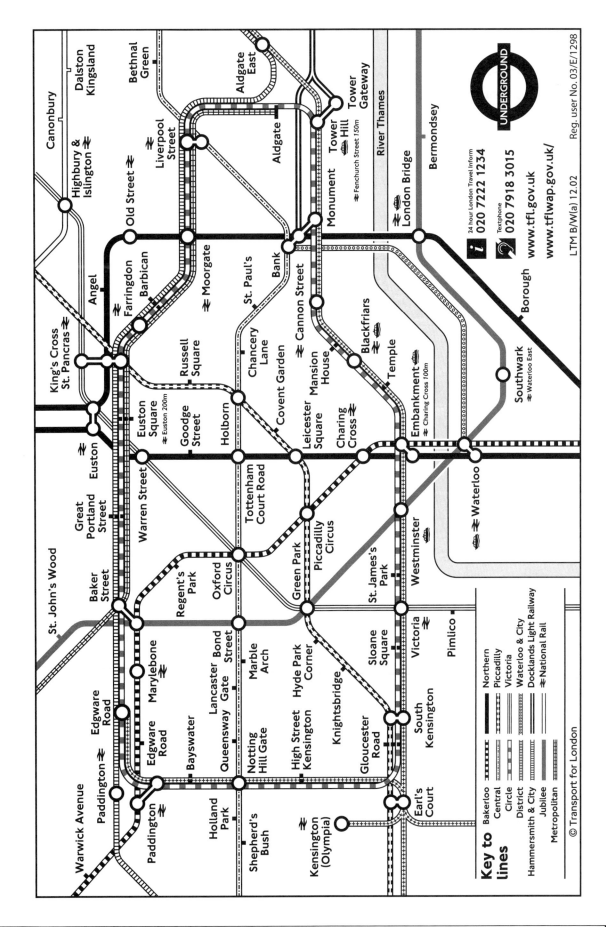

Getting around

1 🎧 The London tube network is very big and has six different zones. Most of the famous tourist attractions are in zone 1, central London. Listen to the pronunciation of these different tube lines and stations in zone 1 and find them on the tube map. Repeat the words with exactly the same pronunciation.

2 Laura and Jamie are at Victoria Station for a day out in London. People have told them about the following places to visit and how much time they need to see each place. Match the places to the pictures.

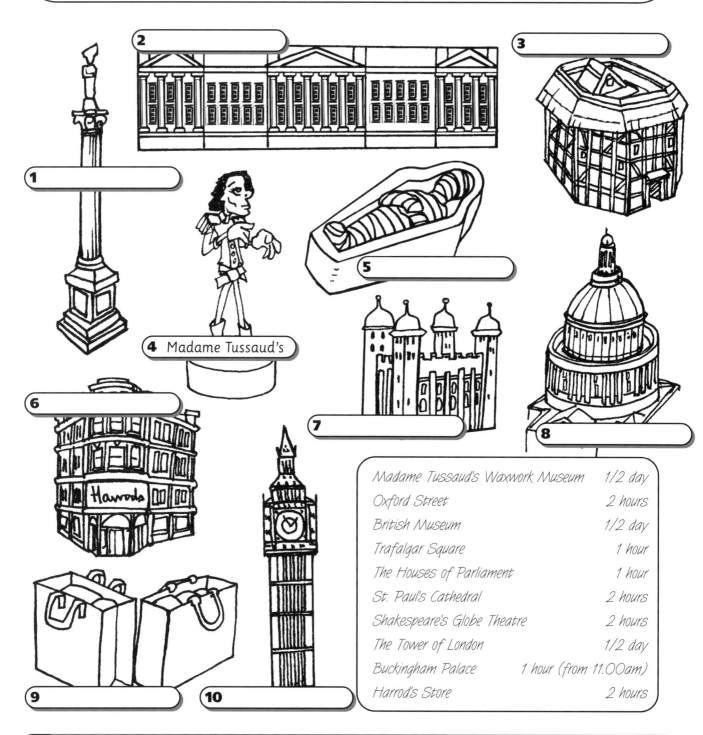

2

3

1

5

4 Madame Tussaud's

6

7

8

Madame Tussaud's Waxwork Museum	1/2 day
Oxford Street	2 hours
British Museum	1/2 day
Trafalgar Square	1 hour
The Houses of Parliament	1 hour
St. Paul's Cathedral	2 hours
Shakespeare's Globe Theatre	2 hours
The Tower of London	1/2 day
Buckingham Palace	1 hour (from 11.00am)
Harrod's Store	2 hours

9   **10**

Getting around

3 How can Laura and Jamie get to the different places by tube from Victoria Station? Use your tube map to complete the following table.

Place	Nearest tube station	Tube line	Change at:
Madame Tussaud's	Baker Street	....	....
Oxford Street	Oxford Circus	....	....
British Museum	Russell Square	....	....
Trafalgar Square	Charing Cross	....	....
The Houses of Parliament	Westminster	....	....
St. Paul's Cathedral	St Paul's	....	....
Shakespeare's Globe	Waterloo	....	....
The Tower of London	Tower Hill	....	....
Buckingham Palace	Green Park	....	....
Harrod's Store	Knightsbridge	....	....

4 Now complete a plan of Laura and Jamie's day out. They want to see some famous sights in London, plus one museum or historical place and they also want to do some shopping. Choose places which make tube travel easy. Don't forget the times to spend at each place!

Laura And Jamie's Day Out:

Famous Sights to see:

....

....

Museum/Historical Place:

....

Shopping at:

....

Plan:

Time	Place	How to travel (tube station and line)
9.00	....	....
....	....	....
....	....	....
....	....	....

5 Now talk about your plan with other people in the class. Do you think there would be time to visit all the places? Who do you think has the best plan?

Notices

① VOLUNTARY WORK
Are you 16 or over?
Do you like meeting people?
Do you like making a difference?
Have you got 3 – 4 hours a week to spare?
Then why not volunteer to help elderly
housebound people by
doing their shopping
decorating
gardening
dog walking
This is very rewarding work that meets
an **important social** need.
For more details **see** Mrs Capstick, Eagle House

② SHOW BULLYING THE RED CARD!
This school operates an anti-bullying
policy. If you feel you have been a victim
of bullying and want to talk about it in
confidence, or if you know someone else
who has been a victim, contact our
school counsellor, Room 82B between
10am and **4.45pm.**

③ SENIOR CHOIR
Do you like singing
with other people?
Are you aged
between 14 – 18?
Want to take it to
a higher level?
We need your
vocal cords!
Lots of fun, friendly
people and the
chance to perform
in public! Come to
a meeting with
Mr Davies this
Thursday at 3.30pm
in the Music Annexe.

④ LOST
Year 11 English coursework folder.
Red cover, with collage design on the
front of famous writers. Desperately
needed for end-of-year assessment.
If you find it, contact me personally
or take it to the school office.
Sam Morgan-Wendell,
Class 5T

⑤ For Sale
One ticket for Strokes gig at Connaught Centre
Saturday 19th October. £20 – includes free lift.
Contact me in class 6C. Jez Marshall

⑥ Want a kitten?
My cat, Comfrey, has had kittens.
Lovely cute fluffy bundles, black,
black & white or tortoiseshell. No
charge, but they must go to good,
caring homes where they will be
well-looked after!!!
See Jan Swirsky in 4E. Only 3 left!

⑧ For Sale
Cricket stuff, incl. bat,
knee pads, wicket,
4 balls. Excellent
condition. A bargain
at only £35 the lot.
Contact Marcus, 5D

⑦ Exchange
Does anybody want to swap Star Wars video collection
boxset (1-3) for any rock and/or metal videos?
Peter Tuck 4B

⑪ Thursday 7th – Saturday 9th November
in the Great Hall
Senior School's Funtabulastic Production
of the hit musical
GREASE
* Cool songs *
* Great Costumes *
* Stunning Dance Routines *
* Hot Live band *
plus
Knockout performances from
superstars of the future!!!
Tickets £4 from the school office
Bring a mate!

⑨ Creative Writing Competition
Stationers & bookseller W.H. Smiths are sponsoring
a creative writing competition open to secondary
school students 12-18 throughout the UK.
The theme of the competition is:
Breaking down barriers
Entries, which can be in prose or poetry, must be
no longer than 2000 words, they must be all your
own work, and they mustn't have been published before.
Send your entry to: Breaking Down Barriers, PO Box 23
Great Boolean Street, Wolverstone, WV1 4RY

⑩ Calling all future Beckhams and Owens!
The Kings Park Junior 11 needs new talent. If you fancy
your form, are free Saturday mornings and on Tuesday
evenings 6.30-8.00 for training, ring Barry Mole on 367060.

⑬ WARNING: ZIP CRACKERS
It has come to my attention that certain students have been bringing
so-called Zip-Crackers into school and letting them off in the playground.
As far as school policy is concerned these 'toys' are in the same **category**
as fireworks and as such are strictly forbidden on school premises **at all**
times. Do NOT bring these crackers into school – anyone caught **using**
them will be dealt with severely.
G. Tunnicliffe, Head Teacher

⑫ FOUND Blue and white Nike 'Megatone'
trainers, size 7. Found in the canteen on
Thursday. Contact Mrs Pritchard in
the School Office.

Notices

> **1** Read the notices quickly and write the correct names in the spaces below. Who should you contact ...

1 if you want to join a football team? ......Barry Mole......

2 if you have lost a pair of Nike trainers? ....

3 if you are caught letting off a 'zip cracker'? ....

4 if you have found an English coursework folder? ....

5 if you have some music videos you want to exchange for Science Fiction films? ....

6 if you want to buy equipment for playing cricket? ....

7 if you'd like to have a kitten? ....

8 if you'd like to help elderly people? ....

9 if you want to sing with other people? ....

10 if you'd like to buy a ticket for the Strokes concert? ....

11 if you are being bullied? ....

> **2** Read the notices again, more carefully. Find the words which mean ...

1 a group of people who sing together ......choir......

2 something you hit the ball with in the game of cricket ....

3 a picture made by cutting out shapes and sticking them onto a piece of paper ....

4 being cruel or aggressive to children who are younger or weaker ....

5 a very young cat ....

6 work (without pay) to help people ....

7 printed in a book or magazine ....

8 another word for *exchange* ....

9 another word for a pop or rock concert ....

10 regular practice (in order to get better) ....

11 what the actors wear during a performance ....

12 the place in a school where people eat ....

13 sticks that burn brightly making a colourful display at night ....

Notices

3 Find the notices that match these pictures a - j.

a ...11....

b ....

c ....

d ....

e ....

f ....

j ....

g ....

h ....

i ....

4 Answer these questions.

1 How much is the ticket for the Strokes concert? ....It is £20.........

2 Where is the Senior Choir meeting? ....

3 What's the name of the musical that Senior School are putting on? ....

4 In which room can you find the school counsellor? ....

5 How old do you have to be to do voluntary work? ....

6 How much are Jan Swirsky's kittens? ....

7 What has Sam Morgan-Wendell lost? ....

8 Which class is Peter Tuck in? ....

9 What size are the trainers which were found in the canteen? ....

10 What does W H Smiths sell? ....

11 When does the Kings Park Junior Football team do its training? ....

12 Why are Zip-Crackers forbidden? ....

A typical school day

1 Look at Laura's webpage and answer her questions about yourself and your school.

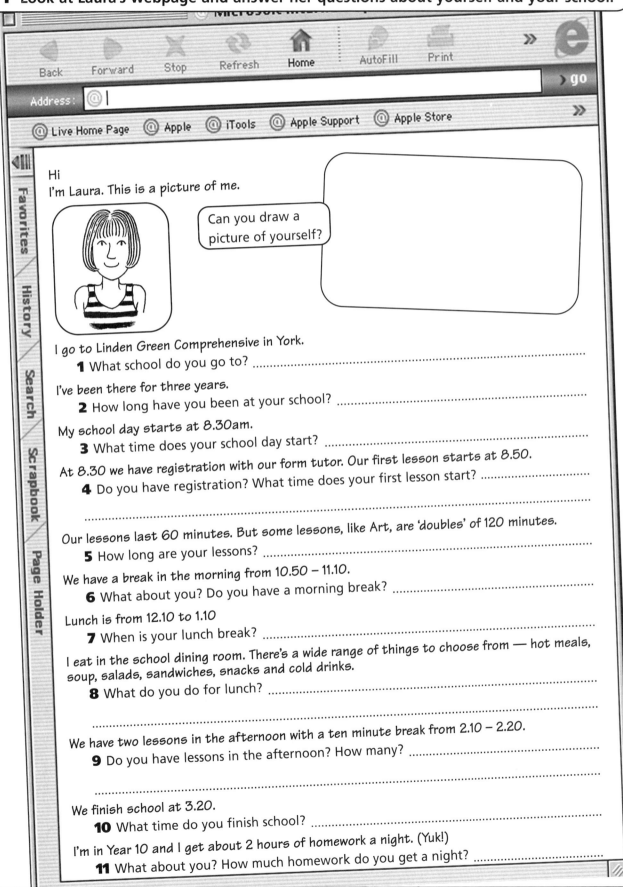

Hi

I'm Laura. This is a picture of me.

Can you draw a picture of yourself?

I go to Linden Green Comprehensive in York.

1 What school do you go to? ....

I've been there for three years.

2 How long have you been at your school? ....

My school day starts at 8.30am.

3 What time does your school day start? ....

At 8.30 we have registration with our form tutor. Our first lesson starts at 8.50.

4 Do you have registration? What time does your first lesson start? ....

....

Our lessons last 60 minutes. But some lessons, like Art, are 'doubles' of 120 minutes.

5 How long are your lessons? ....

We have a break in the morning from 10.50 – 11.10.

6 What about you? Do you have a morning break? ....

Lunch is from 12.10 to 1.10

7 When is your lunch break? ....

I eat in the school dining room. There's a wide range of things to choose from — hot meals, soup, salads, sandwiches, snacks and cold drinks.

8 What do you do for lunch? ....

....

We have two lessons in the afternoon with a ten minute break from 2.10 – 2.20.

9 Do you have lessons in the afternoon? How many? ....

....

We finish school at 3.20.

10 What time do you finish school? ....

I'm in Year 10 and I get about 2 hours of homework a night. (Yuk!)

11 What about you? How much homework do you get a night? ....

All about school

---

1 Read Luke's answers and write the full questions.

Hi!

I'm Luke. I live in Brighton on the south-east coast of England, with my mum, my dad and my younger brother, Callum.

I'm 15 years old. I go to William Cobbett School in Brighton. I'm in Year 11, which means my classmates are between 15 and 16 years old. At the end of the school year, i.e. in June, we have to take G.C.S.E. examinations. The title stands for General Certificate of Secondary Education. These are national examinations and most school students in England take them, usually at the age of 16. I'm going to take 11 subjects. Everyone has to take GCSE in the core subjects – Maths, English and Science and P.E. (that's Physical Education) – and then you can choose from loads of other subjects. I'm doing English Literature, History, French, German, Statistics, Religious Studies and Graphics.

What am I good at? Well, I'm pretty good at Maths and Science but, to be honest, I'm not so great at English. I need to improve my writing. I really enjoy Graphics, though drawing is not my strong point. What subjects don't I like? Well, I used to hate German but now I like it a lot. That's because I've got a new teacher and she's really great. But I'm not keen on History and I can't stand R.S. Actually, to be honest, my favourite subject is Music, but I don't do it at school.

Music is my main hobby. I play drums in a band. We're called Swelter, and our music is sort of indie rock. We rehearse once a week for two hours at the Brighton Music Service Studio. Next Saturday we're playing a gig at the school, so I'm practising hard at the moment (when I've finished my homework, of course!) The noise drives my parents crazy!

1 What's .... *your name* .... ?
Luke.

2 Where .... ?
Brighton.

3 Where .... ?
It's on the south-east coast of England.

4 Which .... ?
William Cobbet School.

5 Which .... ?
Year 11

6 How old .... ?
Between 15 and 16 years old

7 What .... ?
It stands for General Certificate of Secondary Education.

8 When .... ?
At the age of 16.

9 How many .... ?
11.

10 What .... ?
Maths and Science.

11 What .... ?
History and R.S.

12 What's .... ?
Music.

13 Which .... ?
Drums.

14 What's .... ?
Swelter.

15 How often .... ?
Once a week for two hours.

16 Why .... ?
Because I've got a gig next Saturday.

---

2 Read the rest of Luke's letter and then write a reply to him in your notebooks.

Now I'd like to know about your school and what you study. What are you good at? What subjects do you enjoy? Are there any subjects you are not so keen on? Do you have to take any exams this year? What's your main hobby outside school? Tell me everything!

All the best

Luke

Timetables

1 🎧 **Listen to the recording and complete Luke's weekly timetable of lessons.**

	Monday	Tuesday	Wednesday	Thursday	Friday
1			German L2		
2		Science PB Mr			History
3	English A7	Graphics			
4					
5		Science S15 Mrs		Maths P3 Miss	B2 Mrs

TIMETABLE

2 **Write ten true sentences comparing your school week with Luke's.**

Examples:

Luke has Graphics twice a week, but I don't do Graphics at all.

Luke has English four times a week, whereas I have English twice a week.

I have Music once a week, but Luke doesn't have Music at all.

We both have Maths four times a week.

3 **What do you think of Luke's timetable? What do you like about it? What don't you like? Discuss your ideas in pairs or groups.**

Bullying

Bullying

At William Cobbett we believe that our students are entitled to learn in a positive environment. Occasionally, bullying prevents a few children from concentrating on their studies and enjoying school. We are committed to prompt and effective action if this occurs and are confident we can stop bullying. To do this successfully, we need the partnership of students and parents.

What is bullying?

• Bullying is the deliberate, conscious desire to hurt, threaten or frighten someone.
• It can be physical, such as hitting, prodding and pushing
• It can be verbal: nicknames, racist or sexist taunts, personal comments. Students who are new, or different, may be vulnerable. (Verbal bullying is often the most common form in schools).
• It can be non-verbal, such as taking sweets or money, or damaging equipment.

Signs of being bullied: how to recognise it

• Children becoming distressed, not sleeping, not eating, being withdrawn.
• Children unwilling to come to school (stomach aches or headaches).
• Missing equipment for which there is no explanation.
• Children making an unusual request for extra money.
• Bruising, or damaged clothing.
• Change of friendships.

What can you do if you are being bullied?

• Inform a teacher immediately. Victims often believe that bullying cannot be stopped or they are frightened of what will happen if they tell. This is understandable, but wrong. We can act sensitively, and bullying can be stopped when we are told about it.
• Keep a written record or diary of the bullying (who/what/where/when).
• Do not hit back. It will only make matters worse and could blur the real issue.

How can you help us to help you?

• Provide us with details: in order to get away with it, bullies need opportunities.
• Trust us. We know what to do if we have the right information.
• Support us. Both victims and bullies need help to prevent damage to their self-esteem, which can have a bad effect later in life.

1 Read the section called *What is bullying?* and answer these questions.

1 Give two examples of physical bullying. ....

2 Give two examples of verbal bullying. ....

3 Give one example of non-verbal bullying. ....

4 Which types of students are often vulnerable? ....

2 Read the section called *Signs of being bullied – How to recognise it* and find words which mean the following:

1 upset (**d**istressed...........)

2 silent and uncommunicative (**w**........................)

3 things you need for your school work (**e**........................)

4 blue or yellow marks on the skin caused by being hit (**b**........................)

Bullying

3 Read the section called *What can you do if you are being bullied?* and find words which mean the following:

1 tell (**i**.........................)

2 the ones who suffer the bullying (**v**........................)

3 make something less clear (**b**........................)

4 Read the section called *How can you help us to help you?* and find words which mean the following:

1 to escape punishment to (**g**.............) (**a**.............) (**w**.............) it

2 the ones who do the bullying (**b**........................)

3 an injury or harm to someone (**d**........................)

5 In pairs or groups, discuss the questions below.

1 What do you think of the advice given here? Which parts are helpful to parents? Which parts are for pupils?

2 Is it a good idea to keep a written record of bullying? Why/why not?

3 Do you agree that verbal bullying is the most common form?

4 Do you agree that hitting back will only make matters worse?

5 Is bullying bad for the bully as well as the victim? Explain your answer.

5 Now read the conclusion to the text about bullying. Fill each gap with one word from the box.

them   offer   bully   carefully
awareness   where   listening   investigating

William Cobbett School

What Can We Do?
As well as raising (................) through the curriculum and giving students opportunities to talk about bullying in general, we have clear procedures for (................) possible incidents and careful guidelines for (................) to victims, witnesses and bullies. We reassure the victim and witnesses without making (................) feel disloyal, inadequate or foolish. We investigate and monitor very (................) and calmly. We (................) concrete help, advice and support to the victim and take a firm stand with the (................) using appropriate, non-bullying punishment.
Working together, we can help stop bullying.
William Cobbett School is a place (................) everyone can work together, happily and constructively.

School uniforms

🌿 St Catherine's 🌿

School Uniform
All pupils must wear school uniform as defined below:

Girls:
White polo shirt
Green round-neck sweatshirt with
  school emblem (only available from school)
Plain black skirt or plain black trousers
White socks or flesh-coloured, black or white tights
Black shoes (not trainers)

Boys:
White polo shirt
Green round-neck sweatshirt with
  school emblem (only available from school)
Plain black or dark grey trousers
Black shoes (not trainers)

Shirts, trousers and skirts are standard school wear and may be purchased from a number of school outlets.

Boys' and Girls' P.E. clothes
White football/hockey socks
Black or white shorts
Rugby shirt — black with green band
Round-neck T-shirt (white)

The P.E. uniform is available from Dawson Sports, 22 High Street.

All items of clothing should be marked with the student's name.

The following limitations apply:
Shoes with high heels (stiletto or platform) are dangerous in school and are therefore not allowed.
Open-toed sandals or shoes and sling-backs must not be worn.
Jeans must not be worn.
Skirts should be of reasonable length – no mini-skirts.
Only upper school girls are allowed to wear make-up.
Excessive jewellery is NOT permitted:
1 neck chain, 1 pair of stud earrings, 2 finger rings maximum.

If a pupil arrives at school not wearing full uniform, his/her tutor will note this in the pupil's homework diary.

Order forms for school sweatshirts are available from reception or school office.

---

1 Read Leah's email and write a reply to her using the space below.

To: you@school.com
From: Leah@StCatherines.co.uk
Subject: Hi!!
Hi, I'm Leah. I go to St. Catherine's secondary school. As you can see from the regulations, my school has a pretty strict dress code. Mind you, it's not as strict as some. My friend Anna goes to an independent school, and there the pupils have to wear black jackets and school ties. The boys and the girls! And even stud earrings are not allowed. What's it like at your school? What sort of dress code do you have to follow?

....
....
....
....
....
....
....
....
....

School uniforms

2 Read the rules about school uniforms. Then decide if the sentences below are true or false. Correct the false sentences.

1 No girls are allowed to wear make-up.   ( ) true (✓) false

Only upper school girls are allowed to wear make-up.

2 You can buy sweatshirts with the school emblem from Dawson Sports in the High Street.   ( ) true ( ) false

....

3 Girls are not allowed to wear red tights.   ( ) true (●) false

....

4 Boys' rugby shirts are plain black.   ( ) true (●) false

....

5 You are not allowed to wear jeans to school.   ( ) true (●) false

....

6 Jewellery is not permitted under any circumstances.   ( ) true (●) false

....

7 Trainers are an acceptable alternative to shoes.   ( ) true (●) false

....

8 Very short skirts are not allowed.   ( ) true (●) false

....

9 For P.E. you have to wear white socks.   ( ) true (●) false

....

10 Boys can wear dark grey trousers.   ( ) true (●) false

....

11 If a pupil comes to school without the correct uniform, he or she will be sent home.   ( ) true (●) false

....

12 Only girls are allowed to wear high-heeled shoes.   ( ) true (●) false

....

13 Your name must be marked on your school clothes.   ( ) true (●) false

....

Indexes

Level Index

Indexes

Lexical Index

Grammatical/Functional Index

Material written by: Martyn Ford and Dave King

Editor: Katherine Stannett

Designer: Victoria Wren

Cover photos: Bananastock; The Mersey Partnership;
K.Guaida, M.Budney/istockphoto, London Tourist Board.

Cover Design: Victoria Wren

Illustrations by: Martyn Ford and Steve Lillie

We are grateful to the following for permission to reproduce copyright material:
London Transport for the Underground map; Gatwick Airport for the information on
airports; Brighton and Hove buses for the information on bus timetables, Lello Music
Publishing Co./EMI Music Publishing Co. (ASCAP) for 'Girlfriend' by Alicia Keys,
Jermaine Dupri and Joshua Thompson; Sony/ATV Music Publishing UK Ltd. for 'If
you're not the one' by Daniel Bedingfield; Leeds Castle Foundation for the
photograph of Leeds Castle.

The authors would like to thank Laura Bardell for her help and ideas and
Mat Seabrook and Melis Ford for supplying useful information.